IMAGES OF WAR

HITLER'S MILITARY HEADQUARTERS 1939-1945

RARE PHOTOGRAPHS FROM WARTIME ARCHIVES

Ian Baxter

Pen & Sword
MILITARY

First published in Great Britain in 2011 by
PEN & SWORD MILITARY
An imprint of
Pen & Sword Books Ltd
47 Church Street
Barnsley
South Yorkshire
S70 2AS

ISBN 978-1-84884-628-9

A CIP catalogue record for this book is available from the British Library.

Typeset by Concept, Huddersfield, West Yorkshire
Printed and bound by CPI Group (UK) Ltd, Croydon, CR0 4YY

Pen & Sword Books Ltd incorporates the Imprints of Pen & Sword Aviation,
Pen & Sword Family History, Pen & Sword Maritime, Pen & Sword Military, Pen & Sword Discovery,
Wharncliffe Local History, Wharncliffe True Crime, Wharncliffe Transport, Pen & Sword Select,
Pen & Sword Military Classics, Leo Cooper, The Praetorian Press, Remember When,
Seaforth Publishing and Frontline Publishing.

For a complete list of Pen & Sword titles please contact
PEN & SWORD BOOKS LIMITED
47 Church Street, Barnsley, South Yorkshire, S70 2AS, England
E-mail: enquiries@pen-and-sword.co.uk
Website: www.pen-and-sword.co.uk

Contents

About the Author

Ian Baxter is a military historian who specialises in German twentieth century military history. He has written more than thirty books and over 150 periodicals for various military journals. He has also reviewed numerous military studies for publication, supplied thousands of photographs and important documents to various publishers and film production companies worldwide, and lectured to various schools, colleges and universities throughout the United Kingdom and Southern Ireland.

Other books by Ian Baxter

Poland – The Eighteen Day Victory March
Panzers in North Africa
The Ardennes Offensive
The Western Campaign
The 12th SS Panzer-Division Hitlerjugend
Blitzkrieg 1939–1942
The Waffen-SS on the Western Front
The Waffen-SS on the Eastern Front
The Red Army at Stalingrad
Elite German Forces of World War Two
Armoured Warfare
German Tanks of War
Blitzkrieg, Panzer-Divisions at War
Hitler's Panzers
German Armoured Vehicles of World War Two
Last Two Years of the Waffen-SS at War
German Soldier Uniforms and Insignia
German Guns of the Third Reich
Defeat to Retreat: The Last Years of the German
    Army at War 1943–1945
Operation Bagration – the destruction of Army
    Group Centre June/July 1944
German Guns of the Third Reich
Rommel and the Afrika Korps
U-Boat War

Steel Bulwark – Panzerwaffe 1943–1945
Road of Destruction 'Operation Blue and the
    march of the Sixth Army to Stalingrad
    Stalingrad'
Last Years of the Panzerwaffe 1943–1945
Auschwitz – Images of War
Rudolf Hoss – the commandant of Auschwitz
SS of Treblinka
Crushing of Poland
Hitler's Defeat on the Eastern Front 1943–1945
Battle in the Baltics 1944–1945
Hitler's Mountain Troops
Wolf's Lair
Second Battle of Kharkov
Battles of Army Group North 1941–1944
Battle of Army Group Centre 1941–1944
Western Front 1940
Steel Bulwark – Last Years of the Panzerwaffe
    1943–1945
Operation Typhoon 1941
The Last Rally: The German Defence of East
    Prussia, Danzig and Pomerania 1944–45
German Retreat to the Reich
Final Days of the Reich

Chapter One

A Year of Decision

Führersonderzug and Reich Chancellery, 1939–1940

By the summer of 1939 all military preparations for the planned attack against Poland, code-named 'Case White' (Falls Weiss), had been issued to the armed forces. As the second half of August 1939 began, German military chiefs pushed forward their final plans to destroy Poland and liberate its western parts from an area that was predominantly German. On 22 August Adolf Hitler summoned his principle Eastern Front commanders to his mountain retreat at the Berghof on the Obersalzberg and elaborated on his military plans. Speaking with eagerness he told his generals that the war with Poland would be a different type of warfare, not like the dehumanizing years of trench warfare in the 1914–18 war, but a new concept: Blitzkrieg, a swift all out attack of such force and ferocity that victory would be secured quickly and decisively.

As a storm began to brew outside he told his captivated audience that they should display an iron nerve, even if the West wanted war, 'it was vital', he said, 'to crush every living spark out of Poland rapidly and, if needed, brutally'. In one of his most arrogant and uncompromising moods he concluded, 'I have done my duty, now go out and do yours'. Commander-in-Chief of the Army, General Walther von Brauchitsch assured his *Führer* the *Wehrmacht* would do its duty. He then leaped to his feet and dismissed the whole audience telling them, 'Gentlemen to your stations'.

A few days later the planned attack against Poland for 26 August was temporarily postponed. Although the postponement much increased the mental strain and physical pressure on the men waiting in the fields, undergrowth and forests, Hitler and his commanders were confident that when the attack did come, it would be swift and victorious.

Six days later at 4.25am on 1 September, Hitler's Directive No. 1 for the planned invasion of Poland was finally unleashed.

Over the next few days Hitler and his commanders monitored the developments of the invasion from the Reich Chancellery in Berlin. In front of his commanders

Hitler was in awe of the rapid progress of his forces. The campaign it seemed had undoubtedly taken on the character that was to remain for the few weeks that followed. Everywhere north, south and east the Polish front lines were shrinking, cracking slowly but surely under the massive German pressure.

During late morning on 3 September, after receiving the formal British ultimatum of withdrawing German troops from Poland, Hitler told his army adjutant to telephone General Erwin Rommel's protection battalion to expect the *Führer* to transfer to his HQ later that day.

A little after eight o'clock in the evening on 3 September 1939 under the cover of darkness, Hitler's motorcade arrived at the Anhalt railway station in Berlin. Hitler's *Führersonderzug* or *Führer's* special train, which had been moved from the Tempelhof depot, waited on the cordoned off platform preparing for its departure.

At nine o'clock the station's coloured signal lamps gave the all clear and the long train under the command of the stationmaster's whistle hauled out of the platform bound for the battlefield of Poland. On board the train there were nine or more personal adjutants, three or more press officials, several radio operators, a number of guests including the chief photographer, Heinrich Himmler's liaison officer, a representative of the Foreign Office, three valets, the chief driver and a deputy, ten *SS-Begliet-Kommando* men and ten Reich Railway catering service employees including waiters, cooks, kitchen maids and two silver cleaners, five railway-police officers, and three inspectors of the Reich Mail. Two motor convoys were directed wherever the *Führersonderzug* travelled and were available immediately when ordered. A squad of aeroplanes, commanded by Captain Baur, also followed the *Führer's* train.

The train comprised of twelve or more coaches and was drawn by one engine (by 1940 there were two pulling the coaches in tandem). There were among the coaches, two 2cm anti-aircraft wagons, two baggage cars, the *Führer's* Pullman, and one press car with a communication centre including a 700-watt short-wave transmitter. There was Hitler's extensive guest, dining and personal staff accommodation, including a bathing car. In Hitler's personal coach was a drawing room with an oblong table and eight chairs grouped around it. The four remaining compartments of his coach were occupied by his adjutants and man servants. Secretaries, cooks, aides, signal corps men were also quartered in this part of the train. Attached to these quarters was his communication centre, equipped with radio-telephone and several teletype machines. This coach was divided into two, with the other part taken up as a conference room comprising a chair, map and table where Hitler could daily survey the war front. The dining car and sleeping cars could be connected with the postal telephone network during stops. Among the other cars was the escort car for the Reich Security Service or *Reichssicheerheitsdienst* (RSD) and *Führer* Escort Battalion or *Führer-Begleit-Battaillon* (FBB). The remaining coaches consisted of two cars for personnel such as secretaries, cooks, aides, signal corps men, and two sleeping cars for entourage and guests.

During the early hours of Monday morning on 4 September 1939, the *Führer-sonderzug* pulled into a dusty Pomeranian railway siding in Bad Polzin, some 150 miles north of Berlin. Almost immediately a fully mechanized unit comprising of an armoured, rifle reconnaissance and tank company under the command of General Erwin Rommel's protection battalion, cordoned off the area around the train and manned their guns. For the rest of the night the train idled until it was time to move on to its final destination. By dawn the train had moved again and pulled into Gross-Born station, the final stage of its journey.

For the next two weeks, Hitler was to spend most of his waking hours in the stuffy claustrophobic atmosphere of his command coach. In the train, as at the Reich Chancellery, the brown Nazi party uniform dominated the scene. On board there were nine or more adjutants and aides, Keitel and Jodl of the *Oberkommando der Wehrmacht* (OKW) (later, each had his own *Sonderzug*), the *Führer's* army adjutant Gerhard Engel, two personal physicians for the *Führer*, two secretaries, three or more press officers, including the Reich press chief Otto Dietrich, who was soon to write a short book about the journey. There were several radio operators, guests such as the chief photographer Heinrich Hoffmann, a liaison officer of Heinrich Himmler, Karl Wolff, Martin Bormann's younger brother Albert, a representative of the Foreign Office, three valets, the driver and deputy, ten FBB, ten RSD men, fourteen officials and employees of the Reich Railway Catering Service including waiters, cooks, kitchen maids and two silver cleaners, five railway police officers, and three inspectors of the Reich mail. Later Theodor Eicke also operated his command headquarters of the brutal *Totenkopf* regiments from Hitler's special train. It here onboard the train that Keitel introduced to the *Führer* his Chief of Operations, Alfred Jodl. This tall, balding officer impressed Hitler immediately. Jodl was to be his principle strategic advisor until the end of the war.

From the headquarters train Hitler was able to devote his attention entirely to operations in Poland. The train made several movements so that he could more readily visit parts of the front he was interested in. Each day he would appear in the command coach to hear Jodl's personal reports on the morning situation. Four days into the invasion of Poland, which was given the code-name, 'Operation White', the German Army were achieving stunning successes on all fronts.

On and off the train, Hitler took enormous interest in the war against Poland and during every stop the train made, he was able to spend his days, regardless of the risk, touring from the train as a base, moving in two small motor convoys of heavy six-wheeled armour-plated Mercedes vehicles with armoured escort.

On 5 September, the train travelled north-west to Gross Born Troop Training Area south-west of Neustettin; on 8 September, it moved further south to Ilnau, north-east of Oppeln in Silesia. On 13 September it had moved once more and shifted to Gogolin, south of Oppeln. Finally, on 18 September, it changed north again to Goddentow-Lanz, near Lauenburg in Pomerania.

Throughout these tours Hitler's staff continued to busy themselves on board the train with accumulating various reports on the progress of the three armed services. Once these reports had been collected, the daily '*Wehrmacht* Communiqué' was prepared in draft and then sent to the OKW chief of operations, General Jodl, who via Keitel got Hitler's approval and signature. Both the *Führersonderzug* and the Reich Chancellery were in constant contact, continuously exchanging data and other important information, ensuring that the nerve centres were updated and informed, both militarily and politically.

On 19 September the headquarters transferred, for the first time during the Polish campaign from the train to the seafront Kasino Hotel on Nordstrasse in Zoppot, just west of Danzig. There, Hitler occupied rooms 251, 252, and 253 in the hotel. Using this as his base, he continued daily to visit areas of the military operations either by motor convoy or air. Late in the afternoon of 25 September, Hitler returned to his train. The next morning it departed, arriving back in Berlin at 5.05pm on 26 September 1939. Within the hour, Hitler was back in the Reich Chancellery and the *Sonderzug* was parked up at the Tempelhof repair depot.

On 27 September Hitler finally received news that Warsaw had capitulated. The following day the whole headquarters battalion paraded to receive new colours presented to them by the *Führer*. Afterwards, emboldened by the victory over Poland, he assembled in the Chancellery his army and army group commanders and spoke at length about attacking the West. He expressed that Germany must strike as soon as possible, before it was too late. The attack, he said, if conditions were at all possible, should commence during the autumn of 1939. A number of generals present at the meeting had already known about Hitler's intentions of attacking the West during the Polish campaign. Whilst on board the *Führersonderzug* on 14 September, Hitler had discussed the real possibility of attacking the West with his chief engineer, Fritz Todt. He spoke of the need for a proper permanent head-quarters site in the West in which to direct a military campaign. Jodl had instructed his deputy, General Warlimont to investigate ideas for a field headquarters for OKW in west central Germany from which the later phases of the war could be conducted. The headquarters were to be situated out of range of long-range artillery but as near as possible to the Western Front. There was also to be accommodation for the *Wehrmacht* and *Luftwaffe* in the area as well.

For the ensuing weeks to come the search was on for the first permanent field headquarters. General Rommel and some members of his staff looked at railway stations in the west. Hitler's adjutants General Schmundt, Captain Engel, Captain von Below, Captain von Puttkamer, Dr Todt and Albert Speer all scoured the local terrain inspecting possible sites. One suitable location was found by a staff officer of Section L. It was cited in the eastern foothills of the Tauns in the area Giessen-Nauheim, but Hitler subsequently turned down the location. However, the old family estate of Ziegenberg which included a country house and extensive farm land and buildings was finally accepted as the most suitable plot to begin work. The farmer was more than eager to sell the land and alterations for the first *Führerhauptquartier* began almost immediately. Both Speer and Todt were given instructions to modernise the Ziegenberg mansion and this included the construction of some bunkers around the building that were partially below ground level with fortified entrances against possible aerial attack. There were also bunker houses and fortified structures erected looking like alpine chalets with bunkers below ground. Single-storey, pre-fabricated barracks-type housing and wooden barracks clad with thick concrete walls and 4cm-thick bolted windows for splinter protection were also built. Water and electricity were installed along with drains and sewers. Miles of cable pits were dug for the telecommunications, and flak emplacements, trenches and guard houses were sited throughout the installation.

The site was called 'A', for *Adlerhorst*, (Eagle's Nest). By late 1939 work had progressed at remarkable speed with the conversion work at Ziegenberg costing the budget some 3.9 million *Reichsmark*. Yet work on the site had fallen behind schedule and still required more time if it were to be ready to direct military operations against the West. Another worrying problem was the fact that the telephone exchange would not be ready for months. But despite these problems after weeks of extensive work on the area Hitler suddenly announced that he found the new headquarters far too luxurious. In wartime, he remarked, he should live in simple style. As the *Führer* he wanted to have the most modest personal requirements. Those making pilgrimages after the war to his former Western Front headquarters, he declared, would never understand it if he had directed a war in luxury. (It was only at the turn of the year 1944–5, after more than five years of war that the headquarters ultimately came to rest there for the Ardennes offensive. Hitler stayed in the bunkers near Wiesental, which were called 'Amt 500', whilst his Commander-in-Chief 'west' von Rundstedt resided in the Ziegenberg mansion).

In November 1939, another more northern location was found near the little hamlet of Rodert, east of Munstereifel and south-west of Cologne. At about the same time another location in southern Germany was chosen in the Black Forest. Situated near Glans-Munchenweiler the site was nominated, inspected, approved, and work commenced very quickly on the installation.

Whilst the construction and planning of a permanent headquarters in the west continued Hitler's headquarters temporarily resided at the Reich Chancellery. Hitler had equipped the big congress room in his official Berlin residence as a war conference room. In its centre was a large map table. The OKW — Generals Keitel and Jodl moved into the neighbouring rooms vacated by the *Führer's* adjutants.

During the first weeks after the conquering of Poland, Hitler was seen by his war staff anxiously deliberating between continuing the fight against the West and making peace. On 19 October *Oberkommando des Heeres* (OKH) reluctantly issued its first hasty directive on 'Operation Yellow' (The attack on France and the Low Countries). Hitler once again expressed his view that a long drawn-out war of attrition with both Britain and France would be a drain on Germany's limited resources, and expose the Reich to attack from behind by Russia. Whilst Hitler appeared optimistic in front of his staff, among his generals there was an underlying atmosphere of fear and doubt. They did not share Hitler's views and could see no favourable prospect in an offensive. Field Marshal von Brauchitsch did not think that the German forces were strong enough to conquer France, and argued that if they invaded France they would draw Britain's full weight into the war. Other commanders in OKH were also opposed to the plans of invading the West, and personally went to see Brauchitsch, to demonstrate such an attempt. None of them shared Hitler's belief in the new power of the Panzer divisions, and as a result acute differences of opinion began to divide both OKW and OKH.

On 21 November a disgruntled Hitler issued orders to his leading generals and admirals for a special conference at the Chancellery. Two days later at noon a large audience packed the great hall to hear Hitler speak about the opposition to his unorthodox military strategy. For nearly two hours the *Führer* contemptuously reminded his generals that they were to do their duty like every other soldier, and he was determined to stamp out the least vestige of defeatism within its ranks.

Whilst he decided to temporarily postpone the attack in the West, the opposition caused resentment between Hitler and his senior army generals. Consequently, OKW began overriding Brauchitsch's objections and dealing directly with individual OKH generals instead. Keitel dealt with Halder and Jodl with the Army's chief of operations section, Colonel von Greiffenberg. It was Greiffenberg or his senior staff officer, Lieutenant-Colonel Heusinger, who were normally summoned to the Chancellery by Jodl when new ideas from Hitler had to be passed on to OKH. The Commander-in-Chief and chief of staff of the Army now only appeared at the Chancellery when summoned by the *Führer*. Even by the beginning of December there was still no army representative present. Only occasionally did they have to make presentations on matters concerning their services. OKW continued through-out the winter of 1939–40 to scheme against the heads of the OKH and call upon specific generals, even without the Commander-in-Chief's prior knowledge. For instance in a private meeting with the commander of the 16th Army, General Busch, Hitler discussed at length his initial plans for an attack through the Ardennes without ever consulting the Commander-in-Chief. Similarly, Keitel called upon the Panzer ace

General Guderian for detailed advice on the same subject. All this further weakened the Army's position in the *Führerhauptquartier* and prevented it from having a decisive voice on the conduct of any future military operations. Hitler was determined that never again would his military plans be disputed.

In December whilst the War Department busied themselves with plans on attacking the West, Hitler left Berlin for a brief respite at his alpine mountain retreat, the Berghof. On his journey south on board the *Führersonderzug* he spent three days touring the western front joining in the Christmas celebrations of SS regiments, infantry and *Luftwaffe* units.

A few days later he returned to Berlin and again postponed 'Operation Yellow' this time to mid-January. He made it clear to both Keitel and Jodl that if the weather did not clear he would finally agree to call off the offensive until the spring or early summer.

Days later, he was once again journeying south back to the Berghof for Christmas. From this solitary mountain valley known as the Obersalzberg, a lot had changed since work first began in 1935. Visitors now had to pass into an area guarded by a high barbed-wire fence which was almost two miles long and could only be entered following identity checks at two gates. With still no definite *Führerhauptquartier* other than that of the Reich Chancellery, Hitler had been compelled to expand the Obersalzburg. He knew that when he moved from one of his field headquarters to this Bavarian mountain, his whole headquarters would have to move with him including aides, office personnel, signal corps troops, FBB troops and his personal SS body guard detachment, the *Leibstandarte-SS* 'Adolf Hitler'. They all needed quarters and office space so a huge programme designed to house the headquarters was thus put into motion. Part of the alpine infantry barracks at Strub near Berchtesgaden was used and a new camp was drawn up to be built near Winkl, on the Bad Reichenhall–Berchtesgaden road.

In spite of the huge construction programme on the Obersalzburg, Hitler enjoyed Christmas at his snow-covered mountain retreat. On 10 January he was back in the Chancellery and immediately chaired a conference with his senior commanders on preparations for 'Operation Yellow'. Even though weather reports confirmed that everything looked good for an attack, on 13 January bad weather forced Hitler to cancel all movements to the front. Then as the weather increasingly worsened he finally directed that the whole offensive be called off until the spring. He made it quite clear to OKH that a constant state of alert was to be maintained on the assumption that 'Yellow' might begin at anytime.

At the end of January, with plans of an attack against the West looking more imminent than before, Hitler eagerly sent his chief military adjutant on an extended tour of the Western Front. Upon his return to the Chancellery on 1 February Colonel Schmundt excitedly reported that the great General Erich von Manstein and the

Panzer ace General Heinz Guderian had spoken to him about the attack against the West and believed that a decisive victory was possible provided that new methods were applied. The news undoubtedly convinced Hitler of his own military genius and logical planning ability. The subsequent outstanding success of his strategy now made him more reluctant to pay heed to any military advisors. On 17 January he buttonholed Manstein in person when the General attended a luncheon for the new corps commanders. Over dinner Hitler once more spoke about his grand strategy against the West and spoke at length about safeguarding the German war economy in Norway against the British.

The strategic need to occupy the Norwegian coast before the British now began to lay great stress on the war staff at the Chancellery. A special staff had been organized and briefed by Hitler to study a military operation on Norway. Preparations of the operation known as 'Exercise Weser' were studied at length with General Nikolaus von Falkenhorst chosen by supreme headquarters to direct the operation. Once again Hitler gave unprecedented disregard to OKH and did not consult the Commander-in-Chief of the Army at all on the operation. When a staff officer enquired why Halder had not been briefed on the plans Hitler said that he did not wish to overload the high levels of OKH with the Norwegian operations in view of the simultaneous preparations for the campaign in the west.

On 1 March General Falkenhorst submitted his proposals to Hitler at the Reich Chancellery for the invasion of Norway, which now embraced Denmark as well. Two weeks later, on 17 March, Hitler and his staff left the Chancellery and boarded the *Führersonderzug*, now code named '*Amerika*'. Hitler had taken the name of his train from a small hamlet near Gheluvet, south-east of Ypres, near Amerika, where he had first fought in the trenches during the First World War. On board '*Amerika*' Hitler and staff journeyed south to the Brenner pass where he met the Italian dictator, Mussolini to discuss why Italy should enter the war as Germany's ally. Two days later Hitler was steaming back to Berlin. On 22 March he again headed south, flying to the Berghof for the Easter weekend. On Easter Monday he returned to the Reich Chancellery so that he could discuss the imminent military operations with his war staff. At the midday war conference he told his military staff and naval experts including Admiral Raeder that Germany should seize the initiative and occupy Norway by 17 April.

On 1 April, Hitler personally addressed the handpicked commanders who were to carry out the operation. Six days later the German naval fleet were put to sea destined for six Norwegian cities. The naval staff, now familiar faces at the Chancellery, assured their *Führer* they were confident that their task force would yield him victory. By 9 April General Falkenhorst sent a message to the Chancellery with word that both Norway and Denmark had been occupied, as instructed. Yet by the following day reports confirmed that the British Navy were far from defeated and had entered Narvik waters and sunk several German cargo ships and destroyers. The entire German war staff was thrown into complete disarray by the news. The crisis was so bad that Hitler spoke openly to Brauchitsch about abandoning Narvik altogether. For the next week the *Führer* became increasingly agitated by the events that were unfolding in Norway and began to argue with Keitel and Jodl. Even on his fifty-first birthday Hitler was unable to relax as most of his thoughts were immersed in relinquishing the British from Narvik. However, on the last day of April the Chancellery finally received the long awaited word that victory had been secured. At lunch Hitler was in a euphoric mood over the news and thanked Jodl for his contributions to the victory.

Whilst the military crises had thrown OKW into complete disarray, much of the confusion had been attributed to the lack of organization of the headquarters, consisting of many scattered parts. It was acknowledged that Hitler, when the time came to moving to his field headquarters, should employ a new solid organization to direct and exercise an even more efficient system under OKW's operations staff, including an adequate signals network.

Already work on Hitler's new western front headquarters was well under construction. The location for the supreme field headquarters was secret and only certain members of staff from Section L and Hitler's aides were intimately involved in its whereabouts. With the three locations already approved it was the one near the little hamlet of Rodert, east of Munstereifel that was chosen by Hitler. The new site was initially known as 'Installation R', later as 'Installation F', and finally as '*Felsennest*' (Rocky Nest), where Hitler was to direct his campaign against the West. He had already instructed that OKH should be located in the same area, and he personally selected a neighbouring hunting lodge as the headquarters for the Army Commander-in-Chief and chief of staff with a skeleton working staff. The *Luftwaffe* chiefs of staff were left to choose their own headquarters.

Jodl had been given strict instructions to the Todt Organization which were the task of constructing the headquarters, and for the armies neighbouring '*Forsterei*', to complete in the quickest possible time. Now that 'Yellow' was secretly poised to begin in the first weeks of May it was imperative that everything was completed for Hitler at his new headquarters. Whilst the finishing touches were being made to '*Felsennest*', at the Reich Chancellery, Hitler assembled his staff for the last secret conference on details of the offensive in the west. Hitler was informed that the entire *Wehrmacht* had been ordered to be continuously ready to move at twenty-four hours' notice from 5 May. With the German Army now poised along the Dutch and Belgian borders ready to unleash its mighty armoured force at a moment's notice, on 3 May bad weather postponed 'Yellow'. On the fourth it was again delayed. On Sunday fifth meteorological reports again confirmed that bad weather would hamper operations, so the green light was set for Wednesday 8 May instead. On this deadline Hitler told Keitel and Jodl that he was determined not to wait a day longer. He ordered a special time table printed for his headquarters staff. The time table showed his *Führersonderzug 'Amerika'* departing from a little station near Berlin on 7 May and arriving next day in Hamburg en route for an official visit to Oslo. But weather reports confirmed on this day there was still a strong risk of bad weather, so Hitler postponed 'Yellow' and the trip to Oslo. Both Julius Schaub and Martin Bormann were surprised at Hitler's sudden decision to visit Oslo when 'Yellow' was about to be unleashed. Yet unbeknown to them extraordinary security precautions had been taken to keep the location of Hitler's new headquarters secret, even from his personal staff.

During the afternoon of 9 May Hitler and his staff finally left the Chancellery and drove out of Berlin to a small railway station at Finkenkrug. Here 'Amerika' was waiting for them. At 4.30pm the long train with its light flak batteries mounted on flat-top wagons at each end, slowly hauled out of the station into the evening dusk. Concealing its direction 'Amerika' first headed north toward Hamburg, but by early evening it moved south and pulled into a little station called Hagenow. Setting off once more it proceeded south then west to its real destination. By this time members of staff realized that they were not heading for Oslo after all.

Throughout most of the journey Hitler was seen to be outwardly calm, but secretly as the deadline for confirmation of the attack order approached he became noticeably tense and agitated. By late evening, the codeword 'Danzig' was alerted to the troops massing along the frontier to finally order them forward into action.

As the *Luftwaffe* prepared to reach for the skies over the Low Countries an hour before dawn at 4.25am 'Amerika' reached its destination. Through the carriage window the platform sign read Euskirchen; a small town near the Holland-Belgium borders. Security for the *Führer's* arrival was very tight and even a code-word for the event had been arranged: '*Whitsuntide*' (leave approved) signalled the arrival of 'Amerika' at Euskirchen station. Out in front of the station a well armed FBB unit had taken up positions under cover. As Hitler and staff stepped off the train in the semi-darkness he was met by his headquarters motor convoy. For thirty minutes the convoy drove through the rolling countryside, and at 5.00am it finally reached its destination. The area was immediately cordoned off, and Hitler and his staff made their way through the string of security barriers. Passing a high barbed-wire fence through thick undergrowth and trees the convoy made its way up into Hitler's new field headquarters, '*Felsennest*'.

Entrance gate to Hitler's mountain retreat called the Berghof. This was Adolf Hitler's home on the Obersalzberg in the Bavarian Alps near the small town of Berchtesgaden in Bavaria. Hitler was to spend considerable time here during the war, much to the resentment of his war staff. The site was rebuilt, much expanded and re-named in 1935, as the Berghof and was Hitler's holiday residence for ten years. (Bundesarchiv/Hoffman/Kaludow)

A photograph taken just after the New Reich Chancellery building was opened in 1939. In late January 1938, Adolf Hitler officially assigned his architect Albert Speer to build a new Reich Chancellery in Berlin on the corner of Voßstrasse and Wilhelmstrasse, requesting that the building be completed within a year. The building remained his official residence throughout the war and was used as one of Hitler's headquarters when he returned to Berlin. (Bundesarchiv/Kaludow)

Hitler is cheered by a group of *Wehrmacht* and *Luftwaffe* personnel following a tour of the front. He wears his distinctive green leather officer's greatcoat which he wore on many occasions visiting areas of the front.

Hitler's office in the new Reich Chancellery. His office was massive and measured 400 square metres in size. Inside this room he held talks with dignitaries and world leaders and later in the war held a number of war conferences. (Kaludow)

One of Hitler's headquarter guards watches Hitler's aircraft the 'Grenzmark' after it lands. Hitler was the first head of state to have his own personal pilot and airplane. During the 1930s and the Second World War, the *Führer's* special aircraft flew the famous and the infamous including his inner circle and visiting dignitaries throughout Europe, to Hitler's secret headquarters and to the far-flung battlefields of the Eastern Front.

Luftwaffe troops in one of the number of guards houses that were erected wherever Hitler's special train or aircraft arrived or disembarked.

Two crew members pose for the camera whilst sitting on the engine of Hitler's special train code-named before the war as the *Führersonderzug* F (*Führer* special train F). That code-name during the war was changed to 'Amerika' and then renamed 'Brandenburg' from 1943–5.

Hitler's special train. The train comprised of twelve or more coaches and was drawn by one engine (by 1940 there were two pulling the coaches in tandem). There were among the coaches, two 2cm anti-aircraft wagons, two baggage cars, the *Führer's* Pullman, and one press car with a communication centre including a 700-watt short wave transmitter. There was Hitler's extensive guest, dining and personal staff accommodation, including a bathing car.

Hitler during the early part of the war attends a *Waffen-SS* staff luncheon which was held in his honour. During these meetings the *Führer* was able to confer with his men for the battles ahead.

Hitler touring the battlefield. On and off Hitler special train, the *Führer* took enormous interest in the war against Poland and during every stop the train made, he was able to spend his days, regardless of the risk, touring.

Berlin Ahb

Unt Pts 19.12.35
Nächste Unt 19. 6. 36

Hitler on board his special train. From the train Hitler was able to devote his attention entirely to operations in Poland. The train made several movements so that he could more readily visit parts of the front he was interested in. Each day he would appear in the command coach to hear personal reports on the morning situation.

Hitler salutes from his special train.

Hitler has disembarked from his special train with his dog, flanked by his staff and personal body guards he passes his *Luftwaffe* FlaK crew who are saluting him.

A halftrack tows an 8.8cm FlaK gun towards the battlefront during the early phase of operations in Poland in September 1939. The war in Poland was so swift it was nicknamed by the German troops as the '18-day victory march'.

A Pz.Kpfw.I crew pause in their rapid advance through Poland and prepare their tank for its onward drive east.

A variety of vehicles are seen spread out across a field during a pause in the advance through Poland. Hitler regular visited the Polish front from his special train and was regularly informed on the process of his force's movement.

A column of motorcyclists drive along a typical dusty Polish road bound for the front. Note the MG34 machine gun mounted on the side car combination.

A group of motorcyclists pause in their advance and rest before resuming their drive through Poland's heartlands.

A solitary soldier stands next to the work horse of the German Army, the 10.5cm artillery gun, which can be seen positioned under camouflage netting in 1939.

In spite Hitler's insistence that the new art of *Blitzkrieg* be undertaken on the ground by the rapid movement of tanks, much of the German Army in 1939 was still moved by animal draught.

Chapter Two

Attacking in the West

Felsennest, Wolfsschlucht and Tannenberg, 1940

The name 'Felsennest' had been taken from a 400-metre-high wooded hilltop overlooking the hamlet of Rodert. The installation covered some 30 hectares with bunkers and a string of anti-aircraft emplacements with an assortment of barrack-type buildings. In total it had four bunkers with a 250-square-metre floor area and was occupied by two fortified blockhouses and three barrack huts. Some 3,000 cubic metres of concrete were used to construct these buildings. Surrounding the installation was a chain-link security fence with wooden watch towers perched on high wooden legs. Inside the compound, known to its inhabitants as *Sperrkreis I* (Security Zone I) was to live Hitler with his usual entourage of Generals, aides and secretaries from the Chancellery in Berlin. The largest and heaviest building was the *Führerbunker*. Inside Hitler's quarters it consisted of one working room, one bedroom, a few small rooms for aides, and a kitchen and bathroom. Attached to one end of the bunker was a building for his adjutants. At the other end was Jodl's cell. Keitel had a windowless air-conditioned concrete cell next to his. Other structures on site included a barrack-type building hut where the situation conferences were held, and a windowless dining hut that had a long table that could seat twenty guests. On the long wall was a map of France.

From these buildings was a gravel path, which led to a number of various hutments or bunkers. Even the mess was in a pill box. Once inside these buildings there were telephones, switchboards, radios, typewriters, wireless and telegraph instruments. All these buildings served as working and living accommodation, and were virtually undetected from the air.

In the hamlet and surrounding countryside other hut and barrack-type buildings were erected to house all the *Führer's* secondary staff in what was known as Security Zone II. The area had been completely evacuated and a large farmhouse in the village provided adequate working and living accommodation for fifteen officers and clerks, together with some forty ancillary personnel. Some parts of the building, however, were occupied by members of Hitler's personal entourage, including his body guard.

Many of those working in both security zones give a very good descriptive view of life of the entire headquarters. Life in each compound was different in many ways. Officers in Security Zone II were the only soldiers to be seen who led a complete military existence. In the *Führer's* camp, however, it was often characteristic to see many non-military. Those in Hitler's inner circle who were not soldiers wore field grey uniforms, often with badges of rank of their own choosing.

The day's routine in '*Felsennest*' was very much like that at the Chancellery. During various times of the day the three services would report to Security Zone I. Section L collected the reports, sorted them out, added situation maps and then sent them by orderly over to Security Zone I to Jodl, where he would then prepare the briefing which took place in the briefing-room with only Hitler in the chair and his closest staff present. Here at these conferences Hitler and his officers discussed at length the first days of the German Army's attack through the Low Countries, and then France.

At '*Felsennest*' Hitler was in the best of spirits. Commanders and soldiers alike were staggered by the breathtaking events that they themselves had put into practice. As General Kleist's panzers rattled and rumbled victoriously through northern France toward the Channel, on 17 May Hitler left his headquarters and motored to the Bastogne deep in the Ardennes to discuss the progress of the main drive to the Channel with the commander of Army Group A, General von Rundstedt. Before driving back to the headquarters Hitler stayed for lunch and later made an appearance in front of an army unit, appearing exhilarated by the success of his troops. However, upon his return to '*Felsennest*' he became anxious about reports of undefeated forces in France. It was not until 20 May that he was finally reassured that the situation was mastered. That evening during a conference he received a communiqué that panzers had arrived at the Channel coast. Success was now only a matter of time.

During this period of more or less calm at the headquarters there were a number of over flights by enemy planes, but nothing that threatened the installation. Shortly after midnight on 25 May a headquarters anti-aircraft battery opened fire at a plane that flew over the compound. During the next night there was increased enemy activity and 384 rounds were fired by the headquarters anti-tank batteries. Anti-aircraft group Munstereifel reported that a number of aircraft including bombers and small aircraft had been spotted. They fired 570 rounds of MG34 machine-gun ammunition at the planes. At least one aircraft was said to have been hit, where-upon another dropped some bombs but without causing much damage. Over the next few nights further sightings of enemy aircraft were detected with anti-aircraft batteries firing, this time shooting down two bombers in the process.

For the second phase of the French campaign codenamed 'Operation Red', Hitler wanted to move his entire supreme headquarters to the small Belgian village of Bruly-de-Pesch. In May Lieutenant-Colonel Thomas had chosen the village together with

Colonel Schmundt, Captain Engel and Dr Todt. Bruly-de-Pesch was situated some ten miles south-west of Covin, in Belgium. Three hutments were built, one for Hitler, one as a dining hall, and one for OKW Section L. A casino and a few other lightly constructed buildings were built near the *Führerbunker* in a small wood just west of the village of Bruly. The village church and school were used as offices by the headquarters. There was also a second casino and bunker, and a landing strip for the *Fiesler Storch* light observation aircraft, which was located in a meadow south of the village.

The installation was codenamed 'Waldwiese' (Forest Meadow) and was surrounded by barbed-wire barriers and a fixed chain-link fence. Guarding the site were the FBB as well as field guns and ant-aircraft batteries including No. 604 Reserve Fortress Anti-aircraft Detachment. The total strength of the security force was twenty-six officers, 185 NCOs and some 800 men. The troops were supported by six truck-mounted 2cm guns and thirty-five light and two heavy MG34 machine gun positions. This arsenal of weapons was further supplemented by four 3.7cm anti-tank guns, twenty standard 2cm and eight railway 2cm anti-aircraft guns.

Hitler arrived in Bruly-de-Pesch from his 'Felsennest' headquarters on 6 June and re-named the headquarters 'Wolfsschlucht' (Wolf's Gorge). In the early days of his struggle he had been know as 'Herr Wolf', and now he wanted to use this name in reference to the code-names for his *Führerhauptquartier*. Almost as soon as Hitler arrived the village inn was taken over by some of the staff, nicknaming it as 'Wolf's palest' (Wolf's palace).

When the main body of Section L officers arrived by air, the last finishing touches were still to be made to the *Führerbunker*. By a feat of engineering the headquarters was completed on schedule, despite an eight day deadline.

Away from the anti-aircraft batteries and barbed-wire entanglements that menacingly dominated the headquarters, a special garden had been carefully laid out along with gravel paths. By the time Hitler arrived on 6 June the cement of the *Führerbunker* was still wet. The map room was in a local school, Section L officers were in wooden huts but living accommodation was in a country house nearby, since the village itself was occupied by Hitler's immediate entourage. OKH was located some miles away in a small village called Forges in the region of Chimay.

'Wolfsschlucht' was a very modest headquarters. Whilst the staff and security forces used the buildings of the village, Hitler himself occupied a very simple hutment. An air-raid shelter too had been built quickly for him, but he never used it, despite the frequent air-raid warnings.

The *Führer* never really felt at home at 'Wolfsschlucht' as he did at 'Felsennest'. What made it worse were the constant swarms of mosquitoes that relentlessly plagued his building and the surrounding forest. The mood too at the new headquarters was charged with high drama and Hitler appeared more eager than ever to end the war. Christa Schroeder recalled that everyone was impatiently waiting for word that France had fallen. During the daily war conferences reports confirmed that 'Operation Red' had been penetrating enemy lines successfully along the whole front.

During the early evening of 14 June, news reached the headquarters that the first German troops, men of the 9th Infantry Division, had entered Paris. Within an hour, the centre of the city was reached. Only 700,000 of the city's 1,000,000 inhabitants had remained. The rest had taken to the roads south of the city, trying frantically in a vain attempt to escape the clutches of the German onslaught. Three days later on 17 June during a late morning military conference Hitler was handed a message that the French wanted an armistice. One of Jodl's staff officers recalled that when Hitler heard the news he was so delighted he made a little hop. Astounded by Hitler's exhilaration Keitel stepped forward and congratulated his *Führer* telling him that he was the greatest Field Commander of all time. In the afternoon an excited Hitler flew to join his special train at Frankfurt am Main for conference with Mussolini in Munich to discuss the Armistice arrangements.

When Hitler arrived back at his headquarters the terms of the new Armistice treaty with France was discussed and worked out in the church and completed early on 21 June. That afternoon Hitler left '*Wolfsschlucht*' for a couple of days. On the first part of his journey he motored through northern France destined for the forest of Compiegne where the Kaiser's representative Marshal Foch had surrendered to France twenty-two years before. Now in a forest clearing the French would undergo the same indignities as the German Generals did in 1918. Hitler, Goering, Ribbentrop, Hess and von Brauchitsch took their seats on board the historic railway coach whilst the French delegates listened to Keitel reading out the conditions of the Armistice. Hitler was only present to observe the progress of the negotiations and later returned that evening to '*Wolfsschlucht*', master of France.

The following day Hitler secretly flew with Keitel to Le Bourget airport where a column of motor vehicles was waiting to take him to see the architectural wonders of Paris. The next morning they flew back to Belgium.

On 25 June, the Armistice with France was scheduled to go into effect an hour and thirty-five minutes past midnight. During the evening the atmosphere at '*Wolfs-schlucht*' was relaxed. Hitler with his architect, Albert Speer, his adjutants, and secretaries, sat at a bare wooden table in his requisitioned cottage. The lights in the dining room were ordered to be extinguished and the window promptly opened. Sitting in the pitch darkness champagne glasses were passed around. At 1.35am buglers of the 1st Guards Company sounded the cease-fire. Overcome by emotion Keitel rose in the darkness, made a short speech and then raised his glass to the *Führer*, their supreme commander. The generals then stood and clinked glasses whilst Hitler sat filled with emotion. As a courtesy he brought glass to mouth, but never touched a drop.

Over the next few days Hitler's victory had brought a stream of congratulations. Now that victory had been secured, in the last week of June OKW prepared to collect themselves from '*Wolfsschlucht*' and surrounding areas and move deep into the Black Forest on the Kniebis Mountain, near Freudenstadt, in one of the head-quarters prepared in 1939. It was known as 'Installation T' or '*Tannenberg*' (Pine Mountain). On 19 June Hitler had in fact ordered '*Tannenberg*' to be readied for his imminent arrival. Nine days later the *Führer* and what remained of his staff finally left '*Wolfsschlucht*' forever and flew from Gros Caillou airfield to '*Tannenberg*'.

Construction of '*Tannenberg*' had begun on 1 October 1939, and in total some 2,340 cubic metres of concrete went into building two bunkers half sunk in the earth – one for Hitler and the other for communications. There were also a number of barracks and hutment-type buildings erected and a chalet for Hitler, officers and quarters for the OKW leadership, casino, tea house, conference hut, barracks for guards, *SS-Begleit-Kommando* and other security services.

Here at '*Tannenberg*' Hitler had decided on a short stay before returning to the Chancellery so that he could visit the great forts of the French Maginot. This small headquarters was not one of Hitler's most attractively sited installations. The site itself had been built in an area of several acres and covered mainly with tall pine trees. Surrounding the site was a very dense pine forest, which could not be completely cordoned off by a fence or headquarter guards. Most of the buildings were located in the forest, north of the Black Forest High Road. Warlimont's Section L was located more than a mile away in the Alexander schanze *Gasthaus* on the main road, much to the disapproval of the *Führer* because this was outside the Security Zone and posed a threat to security. The landing strip was erected in easy reach of the installation and was in constant use because the OKH headquarters had moved to Fontainebleu.

At '*Tannenberg*' it rained heavily for most of his one week stay. When there was the odd day of sunshine Hitler could be seen walking through the forest of Security Zone I, flanked either by guests, party dignitaries, adjutants or guards. When he was not strolling through the forest taking in the aromatic air, or sitting in the tea house with his intimate circle, his time was spent in the conference hut speaking about the invasion of England. The proposals for the invasion of England were greeted unenthusiastically by Hitler, but none the less he ordered his service commanders to start invasion preparations in the hope that the threat would bring the British government to their senses. His staff also found a site where he could direct military operations against England. A permanent installation had been built in Foret de la Reims in northern France, and the old site at Zeigenberg, was also mentioned. Though Hitler showed no enthusiasm for the site in Reims he did reluctantly agree on Zeigenberg, but still showed no interest for directing a military invasion against England. One evening over at the tea house Hitler openly revealed that he had no desire to conquer Britain or her precious Empire, but to unleash a superhuman crusade against the Bolsheviks in the east.

Whilst the operations staff continued to plan an invasion of southern England, Hitler had a number of private talks with von Brauchitsch, Halder, and Colonel von Lossberg, a member of Jodl's staff, on the possibilities of a Russian campaign. Brauchitsch, Halder and Lossberg said they would immediately go to work on the subject. Lossberg code-named the campaign against Russia 'Fritz' after his son, and ordered the intelligence services to use every means possible to dupe Britain into believing Germany was preparing war against her.

On 5 July Hitler and his headquarters staff finally left the bleak surroundings of 'Tannenberg' and boarded Führersonderzug 'Amerika' for Berlin. With the Führerhauptquartier scheduled to move into the Zeigenberg facility known as 'Installation A' 'Adlerhorst' (Eagles Nest) an advanced detachment of the FBB had left 'Tannenberg' in advance, whilst the rest of the FBB including its commanding officer, Lieutenant Kurt Thomas move in a few days later. Only a small guard unit stayed behind at 'Tannenberg' until 13 July when it was replaced by a guard unit from V Army Corps in Stuttgart. Here the guard unit would remain waiting at 'Tannenberg' for the Führer's arrival.

In Berlin a public holiday had been declared in the capital. Thousands of swastikas lined the thronging streets to the Chancellery, and roses carpeted the roads for Hitler's motorcade. As 'Amerika' pulled into Anhalt station under the sound of a military band, Dr Goebbels himself broadcast the running commentary over the radio network. The arrival of the train was remembered by the headquarters staff as a truly memorable occasion. Many were glad to be back in the capital after spending weeks away. Yet, just three days later on 8 July 'Amerika' was off again carrying Hitler south to Austria and Bavaria. The final part of the journey was Berchtesgaden where he stayed for a week to reflect on his future military plans. Here at the Berghof he assembled his military commanders and grudgingly spoke about the invasion plans of Britain. The code name for the invasion was 'Operation Sea Lion'. Hitler requested that transport ships and their crews were to be moored along the Channel coast in full view of British reconnaissance, and Goering's Luftwaffe were to offer a token force that was evidently unable to secure an objective of fighting for air supremacy.

On 18 July Hitler returned to the Chancellery where he continued to debate launching a cross Channel invasion force, and repeating his powerful arguments in favour of attacking Russia. A week later he left the Chancellery for the Berghof and once again at his mountain retreat held a series of conferences with his OKW, army, and navy chiefs on 'Operation Sea Lion'. He also spoke at length about Russia and instructed his principal commanders that a Russian campaign had to be definitely explored. Due to unfavourable weather conditions it was concluded that the campaign in Russia would have to be launched in spring – May 1941. The Army would then have five clear months in which to defeat the Red Army.

Secretly OKW's operations staff set to work planning 'Operation Fritz', and on 9 August revealed the first directive to begin an eastern build up. Hitler ordered Halder, quite independently of Warlimont's operations team, to prepare the plan of campaign against the Soviet Union. For security reasons, members of staff who were not briefed on Hitler's plans of attacking Russia were made to believe, as was Admiral Raeder, that the growing troop movements transported to the Eastern Front were a vast camouflage to distract from the impending invasion of Britain.

The day Hitler and his staff arrived back at the Chancellery, news reached the *Führer* that Goering's air force had already taken to the skies for England. Over the next few days Hitler and his closest staff busied themselves with its progress. The first reports were a disappointment to OKW. The unpredictable English summer coupled with Hitler's lack of support to the *Luftwaffe* constantly hindered air operations.

On the evening of 16 August, Hitler and his immediate entourage again left Berlin for the Berghof. When he returned a few days later the city had been under attack from British bombers. The days that followed saw Hitler in regular meetings with Goering in an effort to bring about a conclusion to the air war against Britain. Goering was determined to step up the air campaign and asked Hitler if he would lift the long-standing embargo on bombing the centre of London. Whilst the *Führer* pondered on his new execution, Goering left Berlin that afternoon for his new Channel coast headquarters confident that he had the *Führer's* full support.

Whether Goering had been formally advised that Hitler's real ambition was not attacking Britain but Russia, is uncertain. But Jodl's staff certainly noticed that Goering showed absolutely no interest in preparing 'Fritz', believing that an operation of that magnitude would never be carried out. Contrary to Goering's belief, Hitler was serious. He had already found a suitable site for his new Eastern Front headquarters. Todt had been instructed to build the huge fortress which, because of its size and remarkable semi-underground construction would take many months to complete. The site itself, known only by a handful of the *Führer's* closest staff, was situated deep inside the East Prussian forest of Görlitz, a few miles east of the town called Rastenburg. Before the area had been sealed off, it had been a visiting spot for the people in the nearby town. The project of building the headquarters had been left in the capable hands of the *konstrukionburo*, with chief engineer Peter Behrens heading the huge construction team of workers. During this initial construction stage, its identity was camouflaged under the code-name '*Anlage Nord*' (Camp North) and also '*Chemische Werke Askania*' (Askania Chemical Works).

In September, whilst Peter Behrens finalised the blue prints for the *Führer's* new headquarters in East Prussia, Hitler continued dealing with the air war against Britain. During this period the battle over the skies of south east England had intensified.

Unbowed British fighter pilots were staking their lives on a battle regarded by the *Führer* as a half measure. Even as the battle raged and more *Luftwaffe* pilots were being shot out of the sky Hitler was seen by his staff to be more immersed in Lossberg's study 'Fritz', and the first directive re-drafted.

For most of October Hitler was not found at the Chancellery, but on board 'Amerika' devoting much of his time to dealing with politics which took him to France, the borders of Spain and Italy. At the end of October after spending a few days at the Berghof he arrived in Berlin again. In November he once more turned his attention to Russia.

On 5 December the chiefs of staff of the three army groups that were to take part in the planned invasion of the Soviet Union met with Hitler, Brauchitsch and Halder. Now for the first time 'Fritz' became open knowledge in the Reich Chancellery. Those present in front of the *Führer* were well aware how serious the plans for war against their old arch enemy had become. For three long hours they argued through each phase of the coming operations. There is no evidence to suggest that any general objected to Hitler's plans. Everyone gave the impression of being full of genuine enthusiasm for the campaign.

Confident and relieved that he had finally come to the decision to attack Russia, Hitler and his closest headquarters staff boarded 'Amerika' and set off to celebrate Christmas with the troops and *Luftwaffe* squadrons along the English Channel. On 23 December the *Führersonderzug* shunted into Boulogne. As Hitler and his intimate circle sat down to eat in the dining car British aircraft began attacking positions along the coast including the town of Boulogne. The train was hastily moved to the relative safety of a nearby tunnel, but not before the flak crew had a chance to use their 2cm flak guns. Two days later the train spent Christmas day idling on the French coast between Calais and Dunkirk.

For the next several weeks the forthcoming Russian campaign gradually absorbed much of the war staff. During this period the high-level staffs immersed themselves tirelessly in putting together the largest force ever assembled in military history. Numerous generals were seen visiting the Chancellery to discuss the plans. Brauchitsch and Halder were regular visitors.

As the first wave of divisions began moving toward the frontier with Russia, Hitler and OKW were momentarily forced to deal with developments in the Mediterranean where the dreams of Mussolini fighting an independent war had been brought to an abrupt end in North Africa. In a conference with his army and *Luftwaffe* chiefs Hitler felt compelled to send a light infantry and a Panzer division to Libya, with a German Corps staff.

On 6 February, the new commander of the *Afrika-Korps* arrived in the Chancellery. The man briefed to command the operation in Libya was none other than Hitler's old commander of his personal protection battalion, General Erwin Rommel. Bestowed with the formal title of Commander-in-Chief, German troops in Libya, Rommel and Hitler spoke at length about the precarious position of the Italians in the desert.

A few days later Hitler left the Chancellery on board 'Amerika' bound for the Berghof. During his stay he received the first encouraging reports on the progress of operations in North Africa, and did not hesitate sanctioning all Rommel's requests.

With news of the fighting in North Africa going well and British forces being driven from their positions, Hitler and his war staff turned their attention once more to the Balkans. Greece it seemed still refused to offer peace terms to Italy, and it was agreed that the country had to be reluctantly occupied before 'Barbarossa' could safely be launched. The Wehrmacht, however, required a clear road to Greece and whilst Hungary, Romania, and Bulgaria were willing to allow access, Yugoslavia wanted no German intervention in the Balkans.

Throughout March while the headquarters staff prepared itself towards the campaign in the East, Hitler spent most of his time away in the Chancellery trying to persuade the Yugoslav government to heed to his demands and allow troops through the Balkans. By 26 March, Hitler could wait no longer for a political agreement and issued Directive No. 25 for the immediate invasion of Yugoslavia. He told Keitel and Jodl to work out military plans to swiftly occupy the Balkans so that the Wehrmacht could be prepared for the campaign against Russia, even though it had to be postponed by four weeks.

On 30 March, Hitler addressed the first all-service conference of senior commanders earmarked for the Eastern Front at the Chancellery. The conference was so important that Keitel had arranged all the OKW's departmental heads to hear the Fuhrer's address as well. For two hours he elaborated on the ideological and military reasons for war with Russia. He demanded blind allegiance from both generals and soldiers to fight an unprecedented war of ideology. Unlike the western campaigns, he said, the Wehrmacht had to fight in the east with unmerciful harshness.

As he geared his generals for the inevitable showdown in the east the Balkan campaign was finally put into action. On the afternoon of 9 April, German radio began broadcasting the first bulletins on the string of victories in the south-east. Hitler was elated by the news and the following day 'Amerika' steamed its way to Munich. On 11 April, the train made its way to Vienna and then onto Graz. Here a tunnel took a single track railway through the Alps. The OKW command train, 'Atlas' halted on the far side of the 3,000-yard tunnel. Hitler's train stopped before entering the tunnel, near the little mountain station of Mönichkirchen at 7.20am. Although the tunnel to the north of Mönichkirchen had been reserved for the Führersonderzug in the event of an enemy aircraft attack, this never happened and the train was shunted to the station. SS guards immediately cordoned off the area and manned their guns. This heavily guarded area was to be Hitler's headquarters for the next two weeks. 'Amerika' was parked, with the locomotive constantly under steam so that it could at a moment's notice pull into the tunnel. This location was known as 'Fruhlingssturm' (Spring Storm).

Hitler's only real contact with the outside world were the OKW's communications system, the daily visits of his generals and ministers, and showing of newsreels at the nearby *Mönichkirchner Hof* hotel. Apart from this Hitler never ventured from his train beyond the station platform.

From 'Amerika' and the OKW *sonderzug* 'Atlas', Hitler and his headquarters staff guided the Yugoslav and then the Greek campaigns to their victorious conclusion. By 12 April, Belgrade had already been captured, and five days later Yugoslavia surrendered.

On 26 April 'Amerika' left Mönichkirchen for the former Yugoslav frontier. Two days later the *Führer* was back in the Chancellery. Within days he had fixed Sunday 22 June as the new date for the opening of the attack in the east. On 4 May, he assembled his *Reichstag* deputies before leaving the Chancellery once more for the *Führersonderzug*.

Whilst Hitler was away preparatory measures for the invasion continued in all sections of the German headquarters. Under Jodl's direction, Section L carried on collecting the massive amounts of reconnaissance data from the army, navy and *Luftwaffe*. For the usual daily briefings they put forward minor alterations of the plans to OKH so that these could be sent out accordingly to the various commands already in place along the Russian frontier.

On the first day of June, the last stages of the planning were put into motion. The last echelons of German troops were transported from Germany for the Eastern Front. In less than three weeks 'Barbarossa' would be unleashed. On 11 June, Hitler sent Schmundt to check if the new headquarters being built for him in East Prussia was ready. In addition to this new installation, two other sites in the east had also been hurriedly developed for Hitler's use, 'Anlage Mitte' (Camp Centre) near Tomasazow in Poland, and the other was sited north of a railroad between Strzyzow and Frysztak, west of Przemysl in south eastern Poland, and was named 'Anlage Süd' (Camp South). These two installations were merely artificial tunnels of reinforced concrete for the *Führer*, but they were never to be used.

Two days later on 14 June, Hitler returned from the Berghof and assembled at the Chancellery all the commanders of army groups, armies, armoured groups and the naval and *Luftwaffe* commanders together with their senior officers of the high commands of the three services and OKW, with their immediate subordinates. Because this involved the arrival of a very large number of senior officers, Hitler wanted to keep the meeting secret and issued strict guidelines outlining which of the various entrances to the old and new Reich Chancelleries were to be used and times at which everybody could arrive. Those taking part in the conference were divided by sectors of the front into individual groups, and summoned by name to appear at stated intervals, whereupon Hitler warmly greeted them. Those that took part in the meeting with Hitler appeared confident, and when they left the Chancellery later that day were certain Russia would succumb to the mighty blows of the German Army.

On the eve of the invasion the Chancellery was charged with high drama as the *Wehrmacht* was poised along the Russian border. In front of his war staff Hitler seemed anxious, but optimistic. In order to try and relax he retired to bed earlier than usual. Whilst he tried to sleep at 3.00am along a 930-mile front from the Baltic to the Black Sea, 3,000,000 soldiers, an assembly of unrivalled scale and strength the world had never seen before began to inexorably pour across the vast land of the Soviet Union.

In Berlin the news of 'Barbarossa' had roused everyone in the Chancellery from their beds. Later that morning it was confirmed that German spearheads, with their brilliant coordinations of all arms, were pulverising bewildered Russian border formations into submission. For the invasion the German force was distributed into three army groups: Army Group North, commanded by Field Marshal Wilhelm Ritter von Leeb, attacked along the East Prussia-Lithuania frontier, Army Group Centre, commanded by Field Marshal Fedor von Bock, spearheaded his powerful armoured force across the Polish-Russian frontier, both north and south of Warsaw, Army Group South, commanded by Field Marshal Gerd von Rundstedt had been deployed down the longest stretch of the border with Russia. The front, reached from central Poland to the Black Sea. It did not take long before all three army groups sliced through the Russian positions on every front and were driving at breakneck speed through the Soviet heartlands.

The encouraging reports confirmed what Hitler had believed all along. The Red Army had been thrown into total disarray, its infantry resistance was uncoordinated, and its air force almost totally wiped out. Overwhelmed by the initial successes of his army he told his staff to prepare to move to the new field headquarters in East Prussia, where he would direct the total obliteration of the Soviet Army. The move did not come as a surprise to the headquarters staff, and although they expected to be away the longest period of time in any field headquarters thus far, they had been confidently told they would be home before the winter. Nothing was to prepare them for was about to happen.

The bunkers in 'Felsennest', which were covered with straw mats as camouflage. 'Felsennest' had taken its name from a 400-metre-high wooded hilltop overlooking the hamlet of Rodert. The installation covered some 30 hectares with bunkers and a string of anti-aircraft emplacements with an assortment of barrack-type buildings. In total it had four bunkers with a 250 square-metre floor area and was occupied by two fortified blockhouses and three barrack huts. Some 3,000 cubic metres of concrete were used to construct these buildings. (Roger Bender/National Archives)

Map study in the situation room of the OKW barracks. Left to right: General Jodl, Hitler, Major Willy Deyhle, Jodl's adjutant, and Keitel. (Roger Bender/National Archives)

Moving in two small motor convoys of heavy six-wheeled armour-plated Mercedes vehicles with armoured escort, Hitler is seen driving past saluting *Wehrmacht* troops during one of his battlefield tours.

Hitler and Admiral Raeder confer on a path inside Security Zone I at '*Felsennest*'.

(Roger Bender/National Archives)

At 'Felsennest' Hitler on a walk with his naval adjutant, von Puttkamer. (Roger Bender/National Archives)

Hitler on one of his walks, flanked by staff, in the village of Bruly-de-Pesch at his 'Wolfsschlucht' headquarters during the Western campaign in the summer of 1940. (Roger Bender/National Archives)

A column of German vehicles can be seen during the opening phase of the attack through Holland. On 10 May 1940, General Fedor von Bock's Army Group B crashed over the Belgian and Dutch borders. As these unprecedented forces drove on, village by village, town by town, thousands of *Fallschirmjager* and land glider-borne troops were landing on airfields, bridges and fortified posts in order to create a clear path for armour and motorized infantry.

A column of Pz.Kpfw.II advance through France in May 1940. It seemed nothing on earth could stop this stampede of military might from crushing the Anglo-French troops that were being driven along the Channel coast.

A congested road somewhere in France in May 1940. On the ground the German drive through France was undertaken effectively and efficiently. In the air the *Luftwaffe* continued attacking selected targets, mainly going for enemy troop concentrations and bridges.

French troops surrender. British and French commanders struggled desperately to hold their forces together. They were paralyzed by developments they had not faintly expected, and could not organize their forces in the utter confusion that ensued on the battlefield.

German artillery crew in action with their 15cm howitzer. By the last week of May 1940, news was received at Hitler's headquarters that the fleeing enemy troops were being mauled almost to death by constant air and ground bombardments. In the confusion and mayhem that engulfed the British and French lines, the troops were struggling to hold back the Germans.

A German assault team cross a river somewhere in France in late May 1940. Both Hitler and his staff were confounded by the lightning speed and the extent of their own gains during the battle of France.

German troops with their 7.5cm IG18 infantry guns are positioned on a road preparing for battle. During the Western campaign the Germans were far superior in numbers and all their Panzer divisions were intact, with little loss to men or material.

Positioned out in a field during an enemy contact is a 3.7cm PaK gun. The crew is well dug in to protect themselves from enemy fire in the open space.

Troops, which appear to be *Waffen-SS* troops, in action with their 3.7cm PaK gun.

British vehicles abandoned on the beaches of Dunkirk burn. Whilst Dunkirk was regarded as a miracle by the British, it was also one of their greatest defeats in military history.

Chapter Three

The Eastern Front

Wolfschanze, 1941–1942

At first light on the morning of 23 June 1941, Hitler authorised that his special train, *Führersonderzug 'Amerika'* be readied to take him and his headquarters entourage by rail to East Prussia. He also requested that the various echelons of 'supreme Headquarters' follow *'Amerika'* either by rail or air.

The train journey to East Prussia was said to be one of apprehension, but filled with excitement and confidence. Just after midnight *'Amerika'* halted on a local line a few hundred yards from the headquarters perimeter fence. Boarding a column of waiting field vehicles Hitler was driven up to a forest. Deep inside this forbidding heavily guarded wood stood his new headquarters. During the train journey Hitler had called the new Eastern Front headquarters the *'Wolfschanze'*, (Wolf's Lair), which he said, was his code name in the years of struggle.

It was 1.30am when Hitler and staff arrived at *'Wolfschanze'* train station in the heart of the headquarters enclosure. Neither the *Führer* or his entourage were able to see for themselves in the dark the full extent of the newly constructed buildings that covered the installation. Even the dimly lit lamp posts that were dotted along the paths that crisscrossed the complex were unable to pick out the true scale of the place. The installation covered some 250-hectares with an area of some 155,000 square metres of land, with only 4 per cent comprising of bunkers and other structures. All of this was hidden inside the Görlitz forest, and many of the buildings were camouflaged by a Stuttgart landscaping firm which were brought in to plant artificial trees, camouflage netting and various other greenery to disguise the camp.

This was by far the largest of all the headquarters built for Hitler's use and it had taken a considerable amount of labour to construct the site. In total some 5,000 Organization Todt workers had been employed to build the HQ. By the time Hitler arrived at *'Wolfschanze'* there was still considerable OT activity, many labouring night and day trying to complete some of the more important structures. Since September 1940 the OT workers had poured thousands of cubic metres of concrete into the site and erected many buildings to cater for Hitler, staff and personnel, guests, barracks for the guards, housing for the communications centre, roads, paths, railway station, and even an airfield.

It would not be until later morning that other members of Hitler's headquarters staff who arrived by air would see the true magnitude of 'Wolfschanze' and how heavily fortified the headquarters was. To enter the installation by road a visitor arrived at the first perimeter barrier, known as Security Zone IV. This outer perimeter barrier of the installation was heavily guarded by FBB sentries and was manned by three barrier guards. Along the outer perimeter of the forest there were a number of MG34 machine-gun posts and well-camouflaged armoured vehicles and tanks that were positioned at intervals in front and behind the high barbed-wire fence that enclosed an area of about 2.5 square kilometres. Blockhouses, flak and machine-gun towers, and other defensive emplacements including a small minefield also sur-rounded the compound. Even further beyond the outer perimeter was an extensive number of concrete gun emplacements strategically placed at road junctions and covering access roads. Deployed around the installation there were approximately thirty anti-aircraft guns, some seventy light MG34 machine guns, between sixteen and twenty-one tank guns, two heavy MG34 machine guns, and four 7.5cm well-dug-in tank guns. Tanks, mainly of the Pz.Kpfw.III and Pz.Kpfw.IV types, were fully manned and armed in and outside the outer perimeter. During the next construction period of the headquarters two tall bunkers were built to be used primarily as air-raid shelters, barracks for the elements of the FBB manning and patrolling the outer perimeter with its machine-gun and anti-tank gun emplacements, and barracks for the *Führer-Flak-Abteilung* (*Führer* Anti-aircraft Detachment) manning the anti-aircraft batteries throughout the installation. The entire area in and around 'Wolfschanze' including the other headquarters installations were all integrated into the early-warning system of *Air Fleet Reich*, land forces under the control of No.I Military District Command in Konigsberg. 'Wolfschanze', however, was the most heavily defended site of them all. The *Führer-Luft-Nachrichten-Abteilung* (FLNA, *Führer Luftwaffe* Signal Detachment), and a much strengthened FBB (later renamed the *Führer Begleit-Brigade*).

Arriving at this heavily guarded encampment a visitor immediately noticed how well concealed the headquarters were from the road. Once a visitor had been given access through the first outer checkpoint they entered the site. Here they could see a long straight road lined by tall pine trees which led down to the first inner security zone checkpoint, known as Security Zone III. Between the checkpoint barriers of Security Zone III and IV security guards constantly roamed the forest. Armoured surveillance vehicles too made regular daily runs along the road to the outer security ring, along with well-armed troops on foot. At the first inner checkpoint, this barrier was guarded by three or four armed guards and the guard house linked by telephone and radio transmitter. One or two sentries checked the status and passes of the visitor before allowing them through the barrier. Any discrepancies and a sentry could telephone through the details of the visitor to the FBB command post before allowing him through. Here again inside Security Zone III other sentries patrolled the forest and the main road that led to the next inner security zone, Security Zone II. Once again the visitor would then be checked and given access. Within a few minutes the visitor arrived at the checkpoint barrier of Security Zone I, which was the inner sanctum of the headquarters. It was situated north of the Rastenburg/Angerburg tracks and road in the eastern part of Security Zone II. Here sentries manned the western and eastern entrance gates with a barrier, scrutinizing every person that wanted access to this holy compound. It was inside Security Zone I that Hitler lived and planned his conquest of the Soviet Union.

All over the entire installation the HQ was heavily guarded. The OT workers who comprised of many foreign labourers were often scrutinized the most. A Polish labourer called Robert Kowalewski who was contracted by the OT to work inside the HQ between September 1940 and June 1941, said that an FHQu pass was re-quired at all times to facilitate entry into 'Wolfschanze', and a special pass was needed to gain entry into Hitler's Security Zone I, which was known by everyone as the inner sanctum. After gaining access into the headquarters his gang of labourers were never allowed to walk on foot from one part of the site to another, but were escorted by FBB or RSD motor vehicle. All tools and other equipment required to help construct the buildings were checked and signed in, normally by a member of the RSD personnel. Vigilance by the guards was unceasing and the workers often received on-the-spot checks, where passes were checked again. Tools and other valuables were again checked. If ever a workman was to be found walking from one site to another he would be arrested, interrogated and the work foreman called before he was either sent back to his work place or sacked and escorted off the site. In a number of areas if anyone was found walking off the roads or paths, or simply strolling through the forest, this was considered very dangerous as there was a shoot to kill policy.

Almost as soon as Hitler arrived at his new Eastern Front headquarters he went straight to work to try and complete the gargantuan task of destroying the Red Army. Beneath the camouflage netting and inside the huts and concrete bunkers his staff busied themselves. The various huts served as a conference room, mess and administrative offices. Here the military staff monitored closely the developments on 'Barbarossa', as its advanced Panzer units forged ahead victoriously. For this monu-mental attack against Russia the Germans had divided their forces into three Army Groups; North, under Field Marshal Ritter von Leeb; Centre, under Field Marshal Fedor von Bock; and in the South, under Field Marshal Gerd von Rundstedt. The Panzer forces which had been so successful in Poland and France were kept separate from the infantry and concentrated in four independent Gruppen, under the skilful command of Guderian, Hoth, Hoepner and Kleist. They had three objectives,

Leningrad, Moscow and the Ukraine. The Panzer forces were to smash the Russian Army, whilst the infantry and artillery following in the wake of the armoured spearheads were to force the enemies' surrender. It was made clear from the beginning of the invasion that under no circumstances were these forces going to be embroiled in heavy urbanized fighting. The Red Army were to be surrounded by devastating superiority and then destroyed. It was going to be another blitzkrieg victory, but on an immense scale. Within days of the invasion the German spearheads had pulverized Soviet formations along the Russian border into submission. From mid-July German forces were once again engaged in heavy fighting against Russian troops in heavily wooded and marshy terrain around Leningrad.

During August and September further news bolstered Hitler's headquarters. The Fuhrer had become so confident of victory that he ordered his troops in Army Group Centre to commence with the battle of Moscow, code-named operation 'Typhoon', which was unleashed on 28 September 1941.

Confident by the success of the 'Typhoon', Hitler and staff left the headquarters on 3 October for the long haul back to Berlin. Within twenty-four hours 'Amerika' was bearing them back to their East Prussia headquarters.

The next day, Hitler was back at the headquarters and wanting to know the progress of the battle. During October increasing reports confirmed that the Russians were constructing formidable defences in preparation for the German assault on Moscow. At the daily war conference the generals tried their utmost not to show any signs of defeatism, and appeared outwardly optimistic. Yet, as each day passed more discouraging news was received. All along the blazing front the Russians were saturating vast areas with millions of high explosive shells. Hundreds of new truck-mounted rocket launchers concealed under heavy camouflage were being brought into action firing thousands of deadly salvos into an already exhausted and over-stretched German line.

During the daily conferences Hitler and staff had to listen to a catalogue of reports confirming that Bock's Army Group Centre had been badly hit by an unusually early winter. The Russian countryside too had been turned into a quagmire with the roads and fields becoming virtually impassable. On 1 November, 'Wolfschanze' had its first snow shower, and the freezing temperature saw the first heavy snow covering across the entire compound. Whilst the female secretaries found the snow a welcome relief to the normal drab surroundings, to Hitler and staff it was a deep concern. Not only was the weather hampering movement, but the troops were also freezing to death. The German soldier was totally unprepared for a Russian winter. The lack of winter clothing caused widespread worry for the soldiers for they knew that the winter would create graver problems than the Russians themselves.

Throughout November Hitler hardly ventured from his bunker. Other than attending the war conferences he spent most of his time brooding over the battle of

Moscow. During the conferences much of his time was devoted to holding the front at all costs in the face of growing opposition, and combating the worsening weather conditions. As a result of the deteriorating military situation Hitler began arguing more with his generals.

Whilst the Eastern Front stagnated along the frozen plains in the East on 8 December Hitler told his staff that he had to reluctantly leave his headquarters for important business in Berlin. On board the *Führersonderzug* Hitler was seen to be quiet and brooding. Dejection and dismay had spread through the headquarters as the military situation further deteriorated. Just days earlier munitions minister Fritz Todt who had returned from an extended tour of the front told Hitler that given the economic strength of the enemy he could no longer see how Germany could militarily win the war. On 6 December Hitler secretly told Jodl that victory could no longer be achieved. Yet despite the military reverse in Russia, Hitler still showed his iron determination. He told his generals to stand firm until the spring thaw arrived to stave off the Russian offensive. As a result of his fortitude, he categorically refused to permit withdrawal, no matter how urgent his generals' appeals were.

On 15 December during Hitler's return journey back to '*Wolfschanze*' he drafted his first halt order to the Eastern Front, much to the consternation of his army generals. During the conferences that followed there were bitter arguments between Hitler and his commanders, until finally on 19 December the *Führer* relieved von Brauchitsch of his command, who he said, was totally opposed to any halt order. Hitler then announced to a dumbfounded war staff that he would personally take command of the Army in the East and fight the war himself. During a meeting with Keitel he told him that his only major concern to the threat of victory was his generals incessant requests for a withdrawal. For this reason, he confessed, he dared risked leaving his headquarters; fearing defeatism might spread throughout the military hierarchy. It was for this reason he had to act ruthlessly, sacking his closest generals. Bock for one, who had for some time persistently worried him over his constant demands for a general withdrawal, angered him so much during the last week of December, that he relieved him of his command. He was immediately replaced by Field Marshal von Kluge.

Yet, in spite of Bock's replacement, on New Year's eve Field Marshal Gunther von Kluge began telephoning the headquarters, requesting permission for minor with-drawals. Hitler refused outright. That evening supper was served late. Afterwards Hitler fell fast asleep, exhausted at the day's events. As the last minutes of 1941 ticked away, his staff gathered quietly in the mess and waited for him to emerge. But since 11.30pm Hitler had been on the telephone to Kluge listening to him appealing for the freedom to withdraw his troops. For three hours Hitler argued with his Field Marshal, explaining in no uncertain terms the need to stand fast. It was not until 2.30am that Hitler appeared over at the tea house to greet his intimate staff.

Despite the traumatic events in front of Moscow Hitler was relieved to hear that the Red Army finally ran out of steam, and were unable to achieve any deep penetration into the German lines. Undoubtedly this had saved Bock's Army Group Centre from complete destruction. Whilst Hitler was to later say that the battle of Moscow was the *Wehrmacht's* finest hour, his army had in fact failed to capture the city by being crucified by the Russian winter and by fanatical enemy resistance. But much of the failure of Bock's battle to capture Moscow was essentially due to the remarkable Russian recovery, and their winter offensive. The battle had completely altered the *Wehrmacht* from its glorious days in June 1941. Even Hitler himself could not mask the indisputable doubts of the huge task of beating the Red Army, despite his optimism at the war conferences. At mealtimes he appeared tense and uneasy owing to the avalanche of work that had descended upon him since taking command of the Army. Those working with him could see the gradual alteration in his temperament and appearance.

On 10 February Hitler left 'Wolfschanze' and journeyed to Berlin where he took up residence at the Reich Chancellery. When he returned to East Prussia five days later his temperament had considerably altered and he seemed agitated and miserable. Visitors to 'Wolfschanze' saw their *Führer* gray, tired and drawn. In front of his intimate circle he spoke incessantly of the winter crises on the Eastern Front and was particularly hostile towards Brauchitsch and Bock, who he blamed for nearly destroying the whole military plan of 'Barbarossa'. Yet, at the same time, he announced with a sigh of relief that March would bring new beginnings to the war against the Bolsheviks. He revealed that spring would be the foundation of hope for his Army, and concluded that 1942 would see his forces emerge victorious.

As the weather slowly changed at 'Wolfschanze' the daily war conferences saw Hitler openly displaying more optimism for the coming weeks and months. As his health further improved he was quite regularly seen walking along the many foot paths that criss-crossed the installation. On a number of occasions he chatted and gossiped with his staff and even stopped and spoke with the Todt workers who were still labouring daily on the various buildings inside Security Zone 1.

Throughout March there was a gradual German recovery, and as a direct result of this Hitler's health improved. Yet, by the end of the month the spring thaw brought both sides to a standstill as mud jeopardized movement.

On 28 March, a confident Hitler held a three hour war conference where he made use of his army's inactivity. He set out to his war staff a clear list of priorities for the summer of 1942, which he said would commence with a new German summer offensive aimed at capturing Voronezh on the Don. Excited by the prospect of this new summer offensive he told his captivated audience that his armies would drive south westward along the Don to a city called Stalingrad.

Whilst Hitler's war staff busied themselves preparing for the summer offensive in the south, on 24 April Hitler left East Prussia on board 'Amerika' for Bavaria followed by Ribbentrop's special train. Hitler's visit was not to relax at the Berghof, but to prepare for a major speech before the Reichstag.

At the Berghof the Führer was constantly updated concerning the latest news from the Eastern Front. Reports confirmed that General von Manstein's 11th Army was preparing its positions in the Crimea for an all out attack. When Hitler arrived back at 'Wolfschanze' nervous tension gripped the daily war conferences. The meetings with his generals were often heated as the deadline for Manstein's attacked moved ever closer. On 8 May Manstein's force finally opened the attack with a massive air and artillery bombardment followed by an armoured assault. The attack went well and by 15 May some 170,000 Russians had laid down their arms. Three days later the second offensive, code named 'Fridericus' was scheduled to begin with Kleist's 6th Army advancing off the Izyum bridgehead east of Kharkov. However, as Kleist's forces moved into position, the Red Army suddenly launched a surprise attack hurling thousands of tanks and troops into a drive for Kharkov. At 'Wolfschanze' Hitler and his war staff were thrown into complete confusion as Bock telephoned requesting to abandon the 'Fridericus' plan altogether and defend Kharkov. Hitler replied sternly that 'Fridericus' should commence as planned and his generals would have to hold tight and keep their nerve. For five days Hitler brooded over the developments in the south but held the belief that the Russians would be bled to death at Kharkov. By 22 May that abstinent belief became reality. News reached the headquarters that Kleist had successfully linked up with the 6th Army and encircled the Russians. Its success had yielded 239,000 prisoners and over 1,200 captured or destroyed tanks. In front of his war staff Hitler marvelled at the capture of Kharkov and was seen in an ebullient mood.

Emboldened by this victory in the south, Hitler held another conference to discuss the next objective which he code named 'Operation Blue'. It would be here, Hitler said, along the Don and Volga rivers that the Red Army would incur its bloodiest defeat in recorded history.

As his war staff prepared its forces for 'Blue' Hitler returned to Berlin to personally speak to officer candidates. On 30 May 'Amerika' bore him back to Wolfschanze where he discussed further on his bold summer offensive plans.

One month later on 28 June 'Blue' began in earnest. Hitler was seen by Keitel and Jodl to be lively and talkative and full of confidence. That evening over at the conference hut Hitler was handed reports of how the Hungarian divisions had pushed eastwards towards the Don city of Voronezh showing great will and determination against stiffening Russian resistance. By 30 June, General Paulus's 6th Army had begun an all out deep drive southwards towards the Don. Although the offensive progressed accordingly well, Hitler was very concerned about committing considerable troops and precious armour trying to take Voronezh. For hours Hitler argued with his generals about the necessity of reducing the amount of troops being tied to the city. Keitel suggested that his *Führer* fly out in person and order Bock not to take the city.

On 3 July, Hitler made the three-hour flight to Poltava protected by dozens of escort aircraft and hundreds of flak guns along the entire route. Arriving at 7.00am he confronted his disgruntled Field Marshal, and there was a huge argument. During the heated debate Hitler finally gave Bock permission to capture Voronezh, as long as it could be undertaken with the least amount of casualties, and as long as his forces were not drawn into a long protracted urbanized battle. He made it known that he did not want another Leningrad or Moscow.

Later that day Hitler flew back to East Prussia and impatiently watched the operation around Voronezh unfold. By 6 July the city fell, but then unexpectedly two of Bock's armoured divisions were suddenly drawn into a heavy battle as the Russians counterattacked. For two days the battle raged until the divisions were able to withdraw themselves from Voronezh, and then run out of fuel further south. The consequences caused by Bock's military tactics trying to take the city saw Hitler fly into an impassioned rage. He was so angry that he relieved him of his command forthwith.

The *Führersonderzug* at Mönichkirchen, and many of the headquarters staff can be seen outside the train preparing to wish Hitler congratulations on his birthday, 20 April 1941. Headquarter guards can be seen parading.

Headquarters guards parading on Hitler's birthday at Mönichkirchen on 20 April 1941.

A detachment of *Luftwaffe* troops sent to Mönichkirchen to help guard the *Führersonderzug* during its stay between 12–25 April 1941.

Troops and a motorcycle combination advance along a road which has already seen evidence of heavy combat. For these soldiers fighting on the Eastern Front it was often brutal with many areas being fought to the grim death by the Russians. As a result casualties on both sides were massive.

An Sd.Kfz.251 halftrack leads a column of other armoured vehicles and troops along a road which has come under heavy attack. By 1942 the war on the Eastern Front had turned into what Hitler had called a 'war of annihilation'.

Hitler is given a guided tour of his new Eastern Front headquarters in late June 1941. The installation covered some 250 hectares with an area of some 155,000 square metres of land, with only 4 per cent comprising of bunkers and other structures. All of this was hidden inside the Görlitz forest, and many of the buildings were camouflaged by a Stuttgart landscaping firm which were brought in to plant artificial trees, camouflage netting and various other greenery to disguise the camp. (Roger Bender/National Archives)

Hitler's dining room at 'Wolfschanze' in June 1941. (Roger Bender/National Archives)

Teletype office at 'Wolfschanze'. (Roger Bender/National Archives)

Hitler's private office at 'Wolfschanze' in June 1941. (Roger Bender/National Archives)

Telex room at '*Wolfschanze*'. (Roger Bender/National Archives)

The kitchens at '*Wolfschanze*' in June 1941. (Roger Bender/National Archives)

The mail room at '*Wolfschanze*'. (Roger Bender/National Archives)

Duty office of an SS LAH NCO. (Roger Bender/National Archives)

A typical office at 'Wolfschanze'. Note all the wood panelling. (Roger Bender/National Archives)

An interior corridor in one of the huts at 'Wolfschanze'. (Roger Bender/National Archives)

The '*Wolfschanze*' sauna room. (Roger Bender/National Archives)

Mussolini visits '*Wolfschanze*' in August 1941 and is being accompanied from the station by Hitler and Goering.

A long motorcade with Hitler and Mussolini seen in the leading vehicle. SS LAH troops can be seen lining the road.

During a frontline visit on the Eastern Front in August 1941, Hitler smiles as *Wehrmacht* troops rejoice at their resounding success against the Soviet Union. Hitler tells them that victory would soon be theirs. (Kaludow)

A photograph taken in October 1941. Here Hitler confers with his commanders in the map room at '*Wolfschanze*'. During October increasing reports confirmed that the Russians were constructing formidable defences in preparation for the German assault on Moscow. (Bundesarchiv/Kaludow)

Hitler and Mussolini seen here at 'Wolfschanze' station during the Duce's visit in late August 1941. It was during this period of the war Hitler openly confessed to his Italian ally that the war in Russia would be decided at the gates of Moscow. (Bundesarchiv/Kaludow)

A Pz.Kpfw.II moves forward towards the battle front during the initial stages of the war on the Eastern Front. At 'Wolfschanze' everyone watched nervously as reports of 'Barbarossa', the code-name for the invasion of the Soviet Union, victoriously forged ahead. Within hours of the initial invasion of Russia, the German spearheads, with their brilliant coordination of all arms, had pulverized bewildered Russian border formations into submission.

A *Waffen-SS* FlaK crew open fire on an enemy position. By July 1941 the German Northern, Central and Southern Groups had bulldozed their way across vast areas of Russia and were achieving momentous victories on all fronts. In Army Group Centre, both *Wehrmacht* and *Waffen-SS* troops, spearheaded by the 2nd and 3rd Panzer Group, penetrated through Belarussia almost as far as Smolensk, a sprawling city on the Warsaw-Moscow highway.

Waffen-SS troops rest in a field during their exhilarating drive east. So overwhelmed by these staggering successes Hitler was in a relaxed mood in front of his staff, and was more than confident than ever of victory.

Russian PoWs being escorted to the rear following the battle of Kiev in late September 1941. With Kiev captured, the *Wehrmacht* were now in a good position to seize the strategically important oil-producing Caucasus Mountains and the Donetz Basin with its industrialized areas. But in front of his staff Hitler had already been drawing up plans for the resumption of operations against Moscow. He told his generals that the Soviets would be taken by surprise at such an audacious plan so late in the year.

Wehrmacht troops stretcher a wounded comrade to a field dressing station during the opening assault on Moscow, code-named 'Operation Typhoon'. During the early hours of 30 September, the headquarters received word that the first phase of 'Operation Typhoon', had begun. General Guderian's Panzer Group was launched north eastwards towards Orel, from where it would thrust north behind Yeremoneko's Bryansk Front. Two days later, on 2 October, the rest of the Army Group rolled forward.

A 7.5cm l.IG18 infantry gun crew during the drive on Moscow. On the 7 October tension gripped the headquarters at the midday conference as Bock's forces were in the process of completing a huge encirclement around Vyazma. However, as each day passed more discouraging news was being received. All along the smouldering front the Russians were saturating vast areas with millions of high explosive shells. Hundreds of new truck-mounted rocket launchers concealed under heavy camouflage were being brought into action firing thousands of deadly salvos into an already exhausted and over stretched German line.

A 15cm s.IG33 gun during winter fighting on the Eastern Front in 1941. In freezing arctic conditions the entire central front began to disintegrate in the snow. In many areas there was startling evidence that soldiers were reluctant to emerge from their shelters during the blizzards to fight. Hundreds of tanks were abandoned in the drifting snow, and the crews had retreated in panic. In the map room red arrows were deluging every map. An OKW staff officer recalled seeing the situation maps and how the Red Army arrows dominated the overall picture. Dejection and dismay swept the German supreme command.

Wehrmacht troops in the late winter of 1941 pass a stationary Pz.Kpfw.III. At '*Wolfschanze*' the German supreme command were in panic as the German Army in Russia froze to death. Although Hitler said that he had stabilized the front by the end of the year, the damage had already been done. The scars that were caused by the *Wehrmacht*'s failure to capture Moscow in 1941 would be eventually carried to their grave three and half years later.

Out in the snow a soldier can be seen dressed in his winter reversibles looking through a pair of 6 × 30 field binoculars. He is standing next to an MG34 machine gun set up on an anti-aircraft tripod.

Chapter Four

The Road to Destruction

Wehrwolf, Wolfschanze and Wolfsschlucht 2, 1942–1943

With Bock's sacking, Hitler prepared his headquarters staff to be transferred from '*Wolfschanze*' to a newly constructed headquarters site deep in the Ukraine. On 16 July at 8.15am his entire staff left '*Wolfschanze*' and flew in sixteen planes to the new installation, which was situated six miles north of Vinnitsa, just east of the Vinnitsa/Shitomir road. Already, the 1st Rifle Company of the FBB, followed by the 4th Heavy Company, 5th Panzer Company, and Flak Regiment 604, comprising of eight batteries were sent to the Ukrainian headquarters ahead of Hitler.

By midday, Hitler arrived and was greeted by an assorted collection of wooden huts, very different from the concrete bunkers at '*Wolfschanze*'. The site was called '*Anlage Eichenhain*' (Camp Oak Grove), but upon Hitler's arrival he rechristened it '*Wehrwolf*'. The site itself was constructed at considerable cost and covered nineteen hectares of woodland. Scattered across this area was nineteen blockhouses together with *Luftwaffe* and RAD huts for the headquarters staff and security force. Other buildings consisted of a communications centre, hutments for personal adjutants, *Wehrmacht* adjutants, Keitel and Jodl, Chief of Army Staff, Martin Bormann, secretaries, shorthand writers, generals, guests, servants, orderlies, and guards. There was even a tea house, a cinema, bath sauna, and barber. A swimming pool had also been built. Three small air-raid bunkers were constructed as well. One feature that was very different from any other headquarters built was an extensive underground sentry post network for the FBB.

Power to the buildings was supplied by a sub-station. Three diesel generators in a specially constructed building stood ready to supply electrical power if there was any electrical failure. Much of the site was covered with overhead wiring and ground cables for both the sub-station and diesel generator house. Water supply was delivered by two 120-metre-deep wells that had been bored into the ground. Hydrant water was drawn from the River Bug and pumped in to a large tank. Sewage from the installation was drained into a special purification plant inside the headquarters, and miles of pipe and drainage channels led all the way to the Bug.

Work on the Ukraine headquarters had begun in November 1941, and some 8,000 Organization Todt workers together with 1,000 Russians were drafted in to construct the first phase of the site. Following its completion the site looked quite pleasant. However, Hitler and staff hated the place. Nonetheless, Hitler had not come to the Ukraine to enjoy the surroundings, but to direct the German offensive against the Red Army in the south. To help direct the campaign part of OKH also came to the Ukraine from its Mauerwald headquarters and was quartered in Vinnitsa on the edge of the town. At 'Wehrwolf' Security Zone I and II were only a few hundred yards from each other in the open woodland.

For the next three months, Hitler and staff were compelled to live in the Ukraine. Each evening everyone had to swallow anti-malaria tablets. At night it was very cold inside the log-cabins, whilst during the day it was hot and stuffy. The warm air was said to be stifling and this added to the daily rows that were to emanate in the days that followed. Everyone longed for rain and cool weather.

From this new command post Hitler watched with anticipation the German summer offensive unfold. He was optimistic that his forces would soon capture the city of Stalingrad.

Throughout July the climate at 'Wehrwolf' was stifling. Hitler soon began developing headaches and this in turn markedly affected his relationship with everybody, contributing to the constant arguments and the condemnation of his generals, which were to reach unprecedented heights in the weeks to come.

During the second half of July much of Hitler's time was taken-up with the developments in southern Russia. During a conference held on 17 July Hitler received word that two of Paulus's divisions had entered the town of Bobovskaya on the upper Chir. Hitler then immediately ordered that the 6th Army move to the Don bend and hamper any enemy forces that were preparing to build defences west of the Volga. A few days later Paulus received another order from the Führer to take the 6th Army to Stalingrad and capture it by high-speed assault. Paulus, however, did not have adequate reinforcements. His troops too had been marching continuously for almost two weeks and were totally exhausted. But nonetheless he made a determined effort to drive out defences of the 62nd and 64th Soviet armies.

During August, Hitler watched with optimism as news of German forces on the Don poised to strike across to the west bank of the Volga. The drive towards the Volga was almost unhindered by the enemy. By about four in the afternoon on 23 August reports confirmed that the first German troops had finally reached the banks of the Volga, north of Stalingrad. The push on the city now ensued.

In spite the growing resistance in and around Stalingrad Hitler was still seen to be optimistic. However, his health once again worsened. The hot weather coupled with his deteriorating relationship with his generals reached unprecedented heights. Gradually through the rest of his stay at 'Wehrwolf' he began to convince himself that his generals were at the root of all the problems that had escalated on the Eastern Front. Keitel often took the brunt of Hitler's bad mood. Already unhappy in his post, Hitler considered replacing Keitel with Paulus as soon as the General had captured Stalingrad. He also repeated his intention of sacking Halder, who had annoyed him above everyone in his General Staff. General List too was another officer that Hitler could no longer tolerate. During August he had become so perturbed that he told Halder that List was to be summarily removed from his post, so he could take command personally of Army Group A in the Caucasus.

By September his suspicions of his generals became so bad that following a violent argument with Jodl Hitler had decided that never again would his orders be disputed or perverted at the conferences. In future, all briefing conferences would now take place in his hut. A team of *Reichstag* stenographers were immediately flown out from Berlin to Vinnitsa to record every word that was spoken during the conferences.

In spite of Hitler's insistence that every word be taken down during the war conferences this did not deter his General Staff from rowing. For hours Hitler continued blaming his generals for the stagnation on the Eastern Front, and often threw himself into an impassioned tirade in which Halder was made accountable for the military defeats. By 17 September during another bitter argument Hitler finally said he could no longer tolerate Halder and decided to relieve him of his command. A week later Halder was replaced by a forty-seven-year-old commander named General Kurt Zeitler. He arrived at 'Wehrwolf' on 23 September where he met the *Führer* at the midnight war conference. Afterwards, Hitler spoke to Keitel about Halder's sacking and told him in no uncertain words that he ardently believed that with Halder's replacement he had finally stamped out the last barrier of defiance at the supreme headquarters. Now with a new Chief of Staff a spirit of National Socialism would flourish flooding fresh young blood into an exhausted German Army.

Reassured that he had finally found the right Chief of Staff, Hitler left 'Wehrwolf' on 27 September to make another speech in Berlin. Within days the *Führer* returned to the Ukraine where normal routine of the day continued more or less as before. However, at the war conferences the staff noticed that there was an atmosphere of calmness. Unlike Halder, Zeitler was treated with the utmost friendliness, and even Jodl became favourable once more. Between the two men they managed to work out to the *Führer's* satisfaction the daily military operations both in the East and Western theatres. Zeitler was considered to be Hitler's most prominent tactical advisor and took control effectively of the Eastern theatre, while Jodl advised on coastal defence of Europe and other defensive operations in the Western theatre. However, their characters at the war conferences were very different. Unlike Jodl, Zeitler was strong willed and did not take kindly to wild accusations from his *Führer*, and as a result of the new Chief of Staff's nerves of steel his position at the headquarters was firmly secured.

By mid October the weather at 'Wehrwolf' began to significantly change for the worst. Freezing rain would soon bring snow and this prompted Hitler to announce that he intended to leave the Ukraine for East Prussia. On 1 November the entire headquarters staff returned to 'Wolfschanze'. When the staff entered the East Prussian headquarters they noticed that new buildings had been built. Many of the buildings that had previously been erected out of wood were now covered with brick walls and their ceilings lined with concrete in order to protect them against a possible enemy bomb attack. Particular attention was made to protect the Navy liaison offices, a second officer's mess, Jodl's offices, Goering's offices, a cinema, the wooden annexes to the *Führerbunker*, the *Keitelbunker*, and the army personnel office. Once these buildings were reinforced with brick and concrete the outer surfaces were camouflaged with paint, foliage and covered with netting in order to try and conceal them from aerial observation. A Polish labourer working in the installation called Peter Werbewry, said that some of the new buildings were heavily reinforced with concrete ceilings measuring to a depth of two metres thick.

Other buildings constructed were a sauna for the officers, a new tea-house erected near Kasino.l, there was a guest bunker, a number of barracks and bunkers for the *SS-Begleit Kommando*, and officers of the RSD. There was a structure built for the stenographers and a fence topped with barbed wire surrounded it.

Hitler and staff immediately settled down to their normal routine at the East Prussian headquarters. Much of the war conferences were dominated by the events at Stalingrad. Already thousands of German soldiers had been killed or wounded fighting for the city. Although Hitler appeared confident as ever in front of his staff, there were deep concerns that the battle would not end as quickly as initially thought. Over the following days the soldiers of the 6th Army were slowly drawn into a heavy protracted battle of massive proportions. Along the streets, across the roads, inside houses, and factories, the Russians defended to the last bullet. Even when they found themselves cut off on an island of rubble, there was still a stubborn refusal to surrender. As a consequence of the enemies' dogged determination to hold out to the death German troops would spend whole days clearing a street. Although by late September both sides were exhausted from continuous combat, the Germans were very close to gaining control of the southern part of the city.

Throughout October the headquarters followed the unmistakable signs of an army being drawn into a protracted urbanized battle of attrition. Reports confirmed that units were pushing forward into the city and resuming their relentless battle. Through the rubble, twisted steel of factories, shattered and burnt-out wooden houses, cellars, sewers, trenches and holes, they fought and tried to survive.

During November as the battle intensified the atmosphere at Hitler's headquarters became bleaker than ever. Virtually the whole of Hitler's time was now consumed by trying to win the battle of Stalingrad. Stressed and fatigued by the fighting Hitler would drag himself to the conference room and listen intently to whether the fighting had stabilized in his favour.

The days leading up to Christmas 1942 were a sombre occasion for Hitler and staff as they watched Paulus's troops become cut off and surrounded at Stalingrad. The *Führer* no longer joked or smiled, and much of his time was spent discussing the depressing possibility of watching his 6th Army choke to death in Stalingrad. During the conferences Hitler was rarely polite and appeared increasingly agitated as each day passed. His anxiety led to more arguments with his commanders.

Christmas at '*Wolfschanze*' passed with little cheer and even Hitler's intimate staff could not bring him out of his depression. Whilst his commanders continued to press him to order the 6th Army to break out of the encirclement, Hitler believed that Paulus's men were safe inside its 'fortress', and could hold-out until the spring of 1943. He had ordered Goering to increase the air supply to at least 300-tons a day, and thought that this would be sufficient for the 6th Army to survive. But the situation was far worse than Hitler could ever have imagined. His 6th Army was slowly being starved to death. The *kessel* had become littered with thousands of dead, and those still holding out were edging towards total obliteration.

The first bitter days of 1943 opened up as had 1942 – with the German Army facing total catastrophe on the Eastern Front. In the south, where the Germans and allies had deployed the flower of their forces six months before, they were now weakening daily. The Germans exhausted by huge losses, saw a virtually intact Hungarian Army stretching along the Don as probably the only Axis partner capable now of holding the Russians in '*check*'. Along a greatly extended defence line, the Germans supplied the Hungarians with as much equipment as could be mustered.

In the conference room Hitler sat there listening to nothing but a string of problems as the situation in Stalingrad reached new heights. As the headquarters debated on ways to relieve the 6th Army from its entombment, the Russians were already preparing to wipe out the pocket once and for all.

By lunch time on 10 January '*Wolfschanze*' began monitoring reports of a massive Russian attack along the southern and western sides of the Stalingrad pocket. As a result of the attack both the Germans and the remnants of their allies suffered enormous casualties. Hitler told Keitel that he had no doubts that the air of disaster was unanimously approaching. But he still obstinately refused permission for Paulus to break out of the city.

As the last agonising days were played out in the ruins of the city Paulus received word on 30 January that the *Führer* had promoted him to Field Marshal, knowing full well that no German soldier of that rank had ever surrendered. In front of his General Staff Hitler said that he had finally found a brave gentleman who would keep the last bullet for himself, and would never capitulate to the Soviets.

However, as Soviet troops began closing in on Paulus's command post, on the morning of 31 January at 6.15, the radio operator in Paulus's headquarters sent a frantic message saying that the Russians were at the door. Minutes later a German officer climbed out of the command post and waved a white flag to approaching Russian soldiers. Paulus had finally surrendered.

Two days later at 8.40 in the morning of 2 February the last German pocket in Stalingrad finally surrendered. General Strecker's XI Corps had fought courageously for days but was unable to avert the situation decisively. As Strecker's exhausted and starved men shuffled pitifully through the snow into captivity, the Russians rejoiced. The battle of Stalingrad, the most protracted and bloodiest battle of the war, had finally come to an abrupt end.

After the defeat at Stalingrad the atmosphere at 'Wolfschanze' changed forever. Hitler too became a picture of gloom and nobody, not even his trusted female secretaries, could lift him out of his despondency. Those that visited the headquarters during February and March 1943 found the staff depressed and anxious about the coming months ahead. Even those that attended the military conferences found the atmosphere more miserable than ever before. Hitler would often acknowledge his commanders just with a glacial stare, and then murmur to either Keitel or Jodl to proceed with the conference. General Heinz Guderian who had not seen the *Führer* for some time was shocked not only by the pessimism in the supreme headquarters, but by Hitler's appearance. In Guderian's opinion Hitler's physical and mental state clearly showed signs of alteration. During the military briefings he noticed that Hitler was frequently objectionable if one of the staff officers proposed anything that he did not agree with. When arguments broke out he would sometimes stagger to his feet and hurl abuse at the General Staff, and insult the officer that he was speaking to.

Once he had concluded the conference he would leave and retire to his badly ventilated bunker and sit and brood. With his intimate circle, however, he remained uncharacteristically distant and hesitant in his conversation, but never lost his temper. For this reason Hitler stopped inviting guests at mealtimes, preferring to eat alone, or with his secretaries, who were under strict instruction not to mention the war.

In spite the reverberations caused by the loss of Stalingrad Hitler was still fixated with gaining the military initiative in the East. Throughout early February Army Group South had been desperately trying to hold its receding front lines, but many units had already fallen back in disorganised retreat across the southern Ukraine. Perturbed by the receding front in southern Russia Hitler, during the evening conference on 16 February, announced his decision to go to the front and take over command of Army Group South. With him he would take just Jodl, Zeitler, Schmundt, Hewel, and Morell. By early next morning Hitler's motorcade left 'Wolfschanze' for the Rastenburg airfield, bound for the long flight south to Manstein's headquarters.

Hitler's stay at Manstein's headquarters only lasted a couple of days and from there he journeyed to his Ukrainian headquarters, 'Wehrwolf', in order to oversee operations in southern Russia. For the next four weeks Hitler held daily conferences which were taken up almost exclusively regarding Manstein's fervent effort to hold positions in the face of an overwhelming enemy drive. As a consequence the last two weeks of February saw a tenacious German defence, which consequently saw only minor Russian gains made west of Kursk and none at all at Orel. Yet, despite German resilience, both Hitler and Manstein were fully aware that the winter battles had left Army Group Don battered, but still in reasonable shape. Several Panzer units had enough strength to launch a number of counterattacks and Manstein's counter-offensive stiffened by an SS Panzer Corps equipped with Tiger tanks. On 20 February, it fought its way from Poltava back towards Kharkov, thus gaining the initiative between the Donetz and Dnieper rivers.

A few weeks later with news that Manstein had finally restored the Army Groups' position in southern Russia, Hitler decided to leave 'Wehrwolf' on 13 March and head back to East Prussia. He returned that evening to the 'Wolfschanze', after first calling at Kluge's Army Group Centre headquarters in Smolensk. Hitler was informed that the situation in Army Group Centre was relatively stable.

With the southern and central fronts more or less holding the line Hitler flew back to 'Wolfschanze' infused with confidence. Upon his arrival at the headquarters he received more good news that Sepp Dietrich's SS formations had magnificently retaken Kharkov. Hitler for the first time became so excited he immediately telephoned Goebbels asking him to broadcast the good news to the nation, but the Propaganda Minister tactfully decided that it may be best to wait.

Hitler was to spend only a week at his East Prussian headquarters before journeying to Bavaria by his special train, now code named 'Brandenburg'. During the journey at intervals the train stopped, and telephone messages were received. Hitler decided to stretch his legs and took his dog Blondi for a walk outside. Then the train moved off once again. The next morning it pulled into Rugenwalde in Pomerania for a few hours, whilst Hitler inspected Kruppe's new giant gun, 'Long Gustav'.

By the afternoon Hitler was in Berlin and then just after midnight on 22 March, 'Brandenburg' left the Reich capital bound south for Munich. It was here that the Führer's mistress, Eva Braun, joined the train for the short trip to Berchtesgaden.

At the Berghof Hitler immediately settled into the daily routine. His midday conference rarely finished before late afternoon and it was normally 4pm before he emerged to take dinner with his guests. The atmosphere at the Berghof was very different from his permanent military headquarters. Here he was able to transform himself to cheerful host willing to satisfy his guests. Over dinner Hitler often did most of the talking, and then later an adjutant would appear and inform the Führer quietly that everyone had arrived for the evening military conference. Concerned that his guests, particularly the women, would come into contact with the military he asked them all politely to remain seated. It was often gone midnight before Hitler appeared downstairs, drained by the military conference. He would never utter a word to his guests about the briefings with his commanders, but many could see that he appeared optimistic about the future.

For the first time in many months he began showing a growing appetite for a large scale offensive on the Eastern Front, and here at the Berghof he began deliberating such an operation. The new offensive that Hitler had been planning was a big gamble. But he was still confident that he could repeat earlier devastating victories against the Soviet Army. It was at Kursk that the *Führer* was confronted with a very tempting strategic opportunity. Within the huge salient, measuring some 120 miles wide and 75 miles deep, he had been speaking with his generals for some weeks asking whether they could muster up enough armour and infantry to attack from the north and south of the salient in a huge pincer movement and encircle the Red Army. In Hitler's view, the offensive would be the greatest armoured battle ever won on the Eastern Front and include the bulk of his mighty *Panzerwaffe*, among them premier *Waffen-SS* divisions, the crème of his fighting force.

On 21 April Zeitler made a special flight to Berchtesgaden in order to try and convince the *Führer* not to abandon the offensive, drafted as 'Order 6'. A few days later General Model, commander of the 9th Army arrived at the Berghof. In a two hour meeting he presented Hitler with aerial photographs with proof that the Soviets were building strong defensive lines, some of which were impregnable. Hitler decided to cancel the offensive, now code named 'Citadel' until 5 May. On 29 April he again postponed the attack until the ninth, in order to allow more time for additional reinforcements to be brought to the front, including the new Panther tank. When Guderian arrived at the Berghof a few days later he enquired why the *Führer* wanted to start another offensive at all in the East in 1943. Hitler replied that he did have doubts himself, and it made him feel very anxious thinking about it, but he could not let a whole year pass by on the defensive. Guderian said that he needed more time to furnish the front with additional armour before 'Citadel' could be unleashed and that a postponement of at least six weeks would allow sufficient time. Hitler agreed, and on 12 May announced he was flying back briefly to '*Wolfschanze*'. He flew to East Prussia to confer with his commanders on the economic implications of the loss of North Africa. Nine days later he returned once more to his mountain retreat.

Throughout June Hitler immersed himself in the final plans for 'Citadel'. He had been eventually persuaded by Kluge and Manstein to launch the attack. Yet even as the last tank regiments were moving into place Hitler clearly doubted the outcome. In order to keep the attack secret he instructed OKW not to announce the battle publically.

Whilst he received reports of the last troops' movements for 'Citadel', on 1 July after spending almost six weeks at the Berghof Hitler and staff were transferred back to East Prussia. That same evening Hitler addressed his 'Citadel' commanders, who were gathered at Zeitler's OKH headquarters. In a clear confident voice Hitler explained the importance of the offensive, but made it known that the operation had limited objectives. He concluded that he did not want his forces becoming immersed, as they had done at Stalingrad, into a long drawn out bitter battle.

During the early morning of 5 July, 'Operation Citadel' was finally launched with one of the greatest concentrations of fire power of the war. For this daring offensive, the German force were distributed between the Northern and Southern groups, consisting of twenty-two divisions, six of which were *Panzer* and five *Panzergrenadier*.

Over the next few days the battle went well. At the evening conference on 8 July Hitler still appeared optimistic despite reports confirming that his forces had incurred huge losses in both men and weaponry, and deprived the troops of even tactical superiority. During the next few days Hitler was seen to become more agitated by the offensive and increasingly concerned by the loss of large quantities of armour. By 9 July the Russians had managed to ground down many of the *Wehrmacht* units, including those in the SS Panzer Corps, and throw its offensive timetable completely off schedule. It was here on the blood-soaked plains at Kursk that for the first time in the war the Red Army had savagely contested every foot of ground and was finally on an equal footing. Through sheer weight of Soviet strength and stubborn combat along an ever-extending front, the German mobile units were finally being forced to a standstill.

By 12 July with ever increasing losses at Kursk Hitler held an emergency war conference where he decided to abandon the offensive before the entire cream of his *Panzerwaffe* were totally destroyed.

In spite the massive losses sustained at Kursk Hitler was relieved that he had decided to halt the 'Citadel' offensive. Whilst there was a temporary lull on the front he left the headquarters and boarded his personal FW200 Condor and flew with some of his staff to Berchtesgaden, where he would journey to northern Italy to meet Mussolini. Within a couple of days he had arrived back deeply concerned over the Axis alliance with Italy. By 25 July he was informed that the Duce had resigned. Over the next few weeks that followed Hitler devoted much of his valuable time dealing with restoring Mussolini's fascist government, whilst at the same time monitoring events in southern Russia after 'Citadel'.

Following the failure of 'Citadel' German forces were now on the defensive. In the southern sector of the Eastern Front troops frantically withdrew as strong Russian forces smashed through defences and advanced at break-neck speed towards Stalino and Taganrog, along the northern coast of the Sea of Azov. Although German troops distinguished themselves with their bravery, they could only manage to stem the Red Army for short periods of time.

By mid-August, the Russians had wrenched open a huge gap in the German lines west of Kursk, once again threatening to re-take the important industrial city of Kharkov.

Throughout the weeks that ominously followed Hitler and his war staff continued to watch as the German front lines were pulled farther westwards with troops frantically defending, attacking and counter-attacking as the situation demanded. A number of the battles that were fought in this sector of the front were owed to the efforts of Hitler's elite SS formations, but it came with a high price in blood. As the autumn of 1943 approached, a feeling of despair and gloom gripped the German front lines. To many of the soldiers there was a dull conviction that the war was lost, and yet there was still no sight of its end. Being always outnumbered, perpetually short of fuel and ammunition, and having to constantly exert themselves and their machinery to the very limits of endurance had a profound effect on life at the front. During the latter half of 1943 the equipment situation continued to deteriorate, especially in the Panzer units.

At 'Wolfschanze' Hitler tried his utmost to replace and re-supply the massive losses, but it was becoming increasingly futile. Gradually Hitler became more troubled by the deteriorating situation and began blaming his General Staff for the problems. He also blamed his generals for breaking long-distance telephone conversations, and leaks of secret information. Schmundt and NSKK-Gruppenführer Albert Bormann were summoned to the Führerbunker where Hitler told them that he wanted all security measures increased at the headquarters.

Construction style of one of the huts at 'Wehrwolf' in the summer of 1942. (Roger Bender/National Archives)

Entrance to one of the underground bunkers at '*Wehrwolf*' in the summer of 1942. (Roger Bender/National Archives)

The communal swimming pool constructed for the staff at 'Wehrwolf' in the summer of 1942.
(Roger Bender/National Archives)

A Marder on its way to the front lines during bitter fighting on the Eastern Front in 1942. By this period of the war the Germans were striving to find alternatives at combating the ever increasing numbers of the enemy tanks, notably the T-34.

A anti-tank crew prepare their weapon for action against an enemy target.

Goering flanked by two *Luftwaffe* commanders and Keitel looking at a map at '*Wehrwolf*' in August 1942. As the daytime temperatures rose some staff members took to holding meetings outside.

Two photographs showing Karl Dönitz Commander-in-Chief for U-boats. It was Dönitz who ardently believed in the success of the U-boat war in the North Atlantic and, in 1940, he was stationed at Lorient on the French coast. By 1942 he was forced to return to Paris to avoid the growing air attacks on the U-boat bunkers. In January 1943, after Hitler abandoned Germany's ship building programme and concentrated on U-boats, Dönitz was promoted to full Admiral and Commander-in-Chief of the navy, after Admiral Raeder resigned.

SS-Reichsfuehrer Heinrich Himmler views a presentation album entitled, *Grosse Deutsche Kunstausstellung 1941* at 'Wolfsschanze'. *(USHMM)*

Croat leader Dr Ante Pavelic visits Hitler at '*Wehrwolf*'. (Roger Bender/National Archives)

The great march East, troops of the 6th Army push forward during Hitler's great summer offensive, 'Operation Blue'. Hitler had great expectations for the offensive that ended with the objective at Stalingrad.

Hitler can be seen with his back to the camera on a platform watching Himmler greeting Keitel. (*USHMM*)

Waffen-SS troops, more than likely belonging to the crack SS Division '*Totenkopf*' on the front lines with their 15cm sIG.33 howitzer during the winter of 1942.

Troops donned in their winter whites during a lull in the fighting.

SS-Reichsführer Heinrich Himmler at the *Führer* headquarters. Himmler was the architect of genocide and was the Nazi leader most associated with the conception and operation of murdering the Jewish race. Hitler had given Himmler full powers to deal with the wholesale destruction of the Jews, whilst the *Führer* spent his entire time overseeing and planning military operations. The Jewish question was seldom uttered at the *Führer* headquarters, and never with the *Wehrmacht*, *Luftwaffe* or Navy staffs. It was probably only ever with Himmler in private that the two men secretly spoke about the fate of millions of Jews. (USHMM)

SS-Reichsführer Heinrich Himmler with two officers wander along the headquarter's path. (USHM)

Two photographs showing the 'Desert Fox', Field Marshal Erwin Rommel during operations in North Africa in 1942. Until 1942 Hitler looked upon his 'Desert Fox' as invincible in the face of the Allies. However, following the German failure in Africa, Hitler reluctantly conceded that his great Field Marshal would revert from an innovative offensive tactician to a defensive one in Europe. From 1943, the seeds of defeat were well and truly planted for Rommel and further setbacks in Italy and then in France in June 1944 manifested.

With the intensive Allied bombing campaign the Germans built elaborate flak towers in and around many German towns and cities. In this photograph one of the many flak units that were employed to help protect the skies are in action with their quadruple FlaK gun. (*Martin Kaludow*)

Two photographs taken in sequence at 'Wolfschanze', one showing Hitler greeting Dr Joseph Goebbels and the other Ernst Kaltenbrunner. (Roger Bender/National Archives)

Photograph showing Field Marshal Erwin Rommel during operations in North Africa. By 1943 Hitler felt that the Field Marshal had become increasingly pessimistic, and like so many of his commanders, had completely lost his nerve. He told some of his more intimate staff that if it were not for the regrettable succession of events that had transpired, which had prevented him from intervening in time, defeat in Africa would never have begun.

A heavy MG34 machine-gun position overlooking an enemy position during the winter of 1942 or 1943. By this period of time Hitler had become increasingly aware of the dire military situation. The Red Army were now putting up incredible resistance and causing heavy German casualties.

An 8.8cm FlaK gun in action against an enemy target during heavy fighting on the German Central Front.

A Pz.Kpfw.III rumbles along a road bound for the front line. The vehicle still retains its distinctive grey camouflage scheme that was used universally throughout the *Panzerwaffe* in the early part of the war.

A well camouflaged Sd.Kf.251 advances along a road bound for the front. In spite the tenacity of the Red Army to hold its positions to the grim death, Hitler was determined more than ever to crush the Soviets at all costs.

A column of Pz.Kpfw.III have halted on a road somewhere in Russia. The Panzers were compelled to travel great distances across Russia in order to achieve Hitler's grand objectives. As a result of these pressing objectives a number of tank regiments consequently outstripped their supplies, and had no other choice than to halt, or run out of fuel.

Wehrmacht troops of the famous 6th Army march towards Stalingrad during Hitler's summer offensive in 1942. Hitler was determined to smash the Red Army once and for all in southern Russia. As a result of this an ambitious plan was worked out that involved the seizure of Stalingrad, and the isthmus between the Don and the Volga. Following the capture of Stalingrad he planned using the city as an anchor and sending the mass of his Panzer force south to occupy the Caucasus, where it would be used to cut off vital Russian oil supplies. The operation was called 'Operation Blau'.

Soldiers of the 6th Army outside Stalingrad. In the distance parts of the city can be seen burning.

Wehrmacht troops during a pause in the heavy fighting inside Stalingrad. Here these soldiers fought street by street, where vicious hand-to-hand duels were unleashed among the strewn rubble and burning buildings. Although many of these hardened veterans had experienced urbanized fighting before in Russia, nothing could possibly compare to the horrors that they were about to experience.

A soldier leaps from a building. Fighting in Stalingrad was equalled to the horrors of the battle of Verdun during the First World War. However, unlike Verdun where each side rarely saw each other face-to-face and were killed by long-range machine-gun fire or blown to bits by artillery, at Stalingrad the battles were fought separately between individuals.

5cm PaK 38 anti-tank gunners guard an approach along a main street leading into the city centre. As the battle of Stalingrad unfolded Hitler was constantly updated on the progress of troop movements through the city. As the battle intensified all staff at 'Wolfschanze' were talking about the fighting, and became gripped by the developments.

Whilst taking respite beside one of the few wooden buildings left unscathed by the battle of Stalingrad a company commander speaks to his men. By mid-September 1942 more than 40,000 Germans had been killed and wounded trying to take the city.

A photograph inside Stalingrad of a gutted building captured by the 389th Infantry Division at the end of October 1942. Though a number of areas in the centre of the city had been captured the Germans were now drawn into a heavy protracted battle of massive proportions.

Waffen-SS troops during the battle of Kharkov in March 1943. Between 19 February and 15 March 1943, a massive German counterstrike led to the destruction of approximately fifty-two Soviet divisions and the recapture of the cities of Kharkov and Belgorod.

Waffen-SS troops hitching a lift on board a tank following the capture of Kharkov. The capture of Kharkov gave Hitler a tremendous boost in confidence, especially after the destruction of the 6th Army at Stalingrad. In front of his staff he had become more confident than ever that victory in the East could be achieved.

Waffen-SS troops during winter operations in the East in early 1943. Their Sd.Kfz.10 halftrack mounts a 2cm FlaK gun and is well dug-in for action.

Pz.Kpfw.IV's move forward into action during the opening phase of the battle of Kursk in July 1943. It was at Kursk that the *Führer* was confronted with a very tempting opportunity that he was convinced could yield him victory.

At a forward observation post during the battle of Kursk a *Waffen-SS* soldier can be seen with a field telephone. In Hitler's view, the Kursk offensive would be the greatest armoured battle ever won on the Eastern Front and include the bulk of his mighty *Panzerwaffe*, among them premier *Waffen-SS* divisions, the crème of his fighting force.

During the battle of Kursk a *Nebelwerfer* crew are preparing to fire their *Nebelwerfer*. In spite of an audacious start to the battle within five days of heavy fighting many German units had lost immeasurable amounts of men and equipment.

On the front line during the summer of 1943 is a mortar crew preparing to go into action. One of the most impressive mortars used by the Germans on the Eastern Front was the 12cm *Granatwerfer* 378(r).

A squad leader armed with the famous P38/40 submachine gun confers with two of his comrades during a pause in the winter fighting in 1943.

A heavy MG34 machine gun crew in a trench during winter operations in 1943. By this period of the war the Red Army, however, was now in even greater strength than ever before and Hitler's reluctance to concede territory was still proving to be very problematic for the commanders in the field. The persistent lack of strategic direction in the East was causing major trouble too. Nevertheless, in spite of the worsening condition, the German Army, were compelled to fight on.

Chapter Five

Defeat on all Fronts

Wolfschanze, 1944

At 'Wolfschanze' Hitler began the New Year once again fired with optimism. He had convinced the German people to stand fast in the face of adversary and through their iron will and fortitude he promised them victory. In front of his war staff he radiated that same confidence and instilled them with fresh hope and strength of mind. But whatever assurances he gave them the month of January brought nothing but a string of all the familiar problems. By 15 January, news reached the headquarters that the Red Army had unleashed their much awaited winter offensive against the Leningrad and Volkhov fronts in Army Group North. The German 18th Army were outnumbered by at least 3:1 in divisions, 3:1 in artillery, and 6:1 in tanks, self-propelled artillery, and aircraft. By the morning of 18 January the fronts east of Oranienbaum and west of Leningrad were collapsing. The same was happening at Novgorod where a number of German units were being encircled. The Russian Second Shock and Forty-Second Armies then joined the attack against Army Group North. Along the Baltic coast some German elements escaped, but many were trapped and destroyed as the Russians swept in from the east and west. At Novgorod eight Soviet divisions encircled five German battalions. Their one hope was to escape annihilation by hiding in the swamps west of the city. As Novgorod was pulverized into oblivion by heavy Russian artillery, the Forty-Second Army attacked toward Krasnogvardeysk and started battering German units defending the town. The 18th Army was beginning to disintegrate. Fighting in mud and swampland, the troops were exhausted. On 23 January Pushkin and Slutsk were evacuated. General Kuechler, the new commander of Army Group North, appealed to Hitler for a complete withdrawal. During the evening conference Hitler thundered at his generals and responded angrily, prohibiting all voluntary withdrawals and reserving all decisions to withdraw to himself. However, a few days later, after the 18th Army had incurred more than 50,000 casualties, Hitler approved a retreat to the Luga River but directed that the front be held; contact with the 16th Army regained, and all gaps in the front closed.

On 31 January at the noon conference, Hitler informed the Army Group North commander, General Kuechler, that he was relieved of his command. Model, who had been waiting to replace Manstein, was given temporary command of the Army Group. Many of commanders in the field including the soldiers looked upon Model as the *Führer's* troubleshooter. It was Model that ordered his 'Shield and Sword' policy, which stated that retreats were intolerable, unless they paved the way for a counter-strike later. Out on the battlefield Model was not only energetic, courageous and innovative, but was friendly and popular with his enlisted men. Now commander of Army Group North he was given the awesome task of trying to minimize the extent of the disaster that was about to loom along the Baltic. It was here in the north that Model had the greatest opportunity to display his talents as an improviser. He immediately sent out an order to all commanders in the field that they were not to step backward. They were also to uphold the *Führer's* demands that troops were to build defence lines where they stood, and fight to the bitter end.

On 23 February Hitler and his headquarters staff left for Munich whilst the Todt labour force moved in to begin what became known as the last and final phase of the construction programme on '*Wolfschanze*'. Plans had been drawn-up to erect even stronger bunkers in order to safeguard the *Führer* and the rest of the inhabitants of '*Wolfschanze*' from aerial attacks.

When Hitler arrived on the Obersalzburg it was snowing. Camouflage netting covered the Berghof, and the sunlight was restricted through the famous windows of the great hall. Most of the staff found life at the Berghof as isolating as at '*Wolfschanze*'. Hitler, however, appeared more relaxed.

On 30 March the *Führer* sent his Condor aircraft to Lwow to collect two field marshals. Just before the evening conference Hitler met Manstein and handed him the Swords to his Knights Cross and announced that he had decided to place the Army Group in other hands. For the arduous task now pending he had chosen Model as the suitable candidate to take charge of the Army Group. Both Hitler and Manstein shook hands and departed. Model was already waiting outside with General Kleist's successor, General Ferdinand Schorner.

A week later bad news arrived at the Berghof. The headquarters had been monitoring closely the escalating fighting in southern Russia, and on 8 April a grim and bloody battle began to rage in the Crimea. Zietler appealed for a withdrawal, but Hitler flatly refused to permit the evacuation from the peninsula. In spite Schorner's new appointment to southern Russia events there were now moving faster than Hitler's orders. At the General's command post he sent word to the Berghof that a bold fierce all-out attack by thousands of Red Army troops had begun and stormed and penetrated the Sevastopol fortress. By 8 May supreme headquarters reluctantly conceded defeat and Hitler ordered the evacuation by sea of the 17th Army.

Whilst the Eastern Front offered no reassurances of stability from the growing might of the Red Army, in the west Hitler was becoming increasingly uneasy about German intelligence services picking up radio traffic regarding an imminent Anglo-American invasion. By late May and early June German code-breaking radio monitors were still deciphering endless BBC radio traffic through to the OKW. It was believed that Normandy and Brittany would be the probable landing site, but only as a diversionary tactic prior to the main operation across the straits of Dover.

When Hitler finally retired from his midnight conference during the early hours of 6 June he did not suspect that a huge armada of 5,000 ships laden with the enemy was at that very moment approaching the coast line of Normandy. By the time Hitler awoke at 9.00am the Battle of Normandy was already in full swing. In his dressing gown Hitler was handed the latest reports and sent for Keitel and Jodl. When they arrived he was annoyed that the various command centres were unaware of exactly where the main invasion strike would take place. Both Keitel and Jodl, and indeed much of the General Staff, were convinced that the Normandy landings were a diversionary tactic prior to the main landings at Calais. It was for this reason Hitler dared not throw everything he had in France into the Normandy battle.

By 10 June the atmosphere at the Berghof deteriorated further as reports revealed that the enemy could not be contained along the shores of northern France. A week later, with the battle of France escalating on the night of 16 June four Focke-Wulf Condors flew Hitler and staff to France, while the entire *Luftwaffe* along the way was grounded and ant-aircraft batteries were ordered to cease firing. The next morning Hitler's motorcade drove to '*Wolfsschlucht 2*', an unused *Führer* headquarters between Soissons and Laon.

Work had begun on the complex in late 1942. The main part of the site comprised of a railway tunnel which was fitted with armoured sliding doors that retracted into the rock walls. Large bunkers were built into the hillside and the walls and ceilings were up to 3.5 metres thick. The main bunker constructed was the *Führerbunker*. This building had a 90-square-metre hall and dog kennels. A flight of stairs led down to a bomb-proof air-raid shelter.

The whole area was heavily defended by guards of the FBB. Control posts, field patrols and fixed sentry points ensured that there would be no unauthorized entry into the compound. At fixed intervals there were armoured vehicles and MG34 and MG42 machine-gun posts. A ring of anti-tank and anti-aircraft battery emplacements protected both the ground and air from possible attack. Seven heavy anti-aircraft batteries, each equipped with the deadly 8.8cm FlaK gun surrounded the head-quarters, and were supported by twenty-one light and medium AA emplacements and eighteen searchlight batteries.

The headquarters had a telephone and telex circuits and each operator served a switchboard that was capable of managing nearly 100 connections. The telephone system was ample for the temporary use of the site.

When Hitler arrived at the heavily guarded enclosure he met Rommel and Rundstedt. With total frankness Rommel briefed Hitler on the overwhelming threat of the allies and the dwindling forces in Normandy. The troops, he said, were defending courageously, even the seventeen and eighteen year olds. But against the enormous might of the enemy it would be only a matter of days before the front collapsed. Whilst Rundstedt briefed the *Führer* on the situation an air raid warning forced adjournment to the underground concrete bunker. Rommel once again continued to discuss the deplorable military situation, and then they took a brief break for lunch. To the astonishment of Rommel during lunch two SS guards stood over the *Führer* testing his plate of rice and vegetables before he would take a bite. This was visible proof of Hitler's distrust of the officer corps.

Hitler's visit to 'W2' lasted less than twenty-four hours and within a couple of days he was back at the Berghof. Up at his mountain retreat he was torn between remaining in Bavaria and overseeing developments in France, or returning to '*Wolfschanze*' and fighting the war in the East. Yet, a few days later on 22 June, the third anniversary of the German invasion of the Soviet Union, he received worrying reports that the Red Army had marked the occasion with the largest offensive of the war. The attack was so great that supreme headquarters were thrown into total confusion. Within a week Army Group Centre was almost decimated.

General Busch reported that the 9th Army was significantly damaged with high losses, the 4th Army was retreating, and the 3rd Panzer Army was in a critical state with one corps left out of its original three. The entire front of Army Group Centre had been pierced in numerous places and although considerable numbers of troops were trying to hold their defensive positions, they were unable to avoid the encirclements. Nevertheless, Busch was determined to execute the *Führer's* Operations Order 8, which had demanded that all three armies immediately stop withdrawing and hold a new line due north and south of Berezina. Busch wasted no time and instructed the three armies to halt, but the damage to them was far beyond repair.

With nothing but a string of defeats Hitler decided to finally replace Busch with Field Marshal Model in order to instill new vigour and restore determination into Army Group Centre. The change in command pleased many of the commanders in the Army Group. Many of them had been bitter over the developments, which had resulted in the way that Army Group Centre had been led. General Nikolaus Vormann for one, who had replaced General Jordan as Commander-in-General, received the news with 'satisfaction and renewed confidence'. Many of the commanders in the field including the soldiers looked upon Model as the *Führer's* troubleshooter. He had been the commander who had first introduced in early 1944 the 'Shield and Sword' policy on the Eastern Front, which stated that retreats were intolerable, unless they paved the way for a counterstrike later.

On 15 July Hitler returned once more to 'Wolfschanze'. Upon his arrival he found that the installation had changed considerably, especially in Security Zone I. Many of the previous wooden structures were now brick and concrete reinforced structures. Thousands of tons of concrete had been poured into these buildings, and particular attention had been made to reinforce Keitel, Goering, and the Bormann bunkers. Other buildings too were given additional concrete and bricks to help safeguard them against possible aerial attack. Hitler's bunker had still not been completed, and all his furniture including bed and office was moved temporarily over to the Guest Bunker. The Guest Bunker was roomy, but not to Hitler's liking and he could not sleep properly. During the day he could hear Todt workers with pneumatic drills and other tools, but when he left his bunker to stroll across to the conference room he was regularly seen to stop and chat with the workers, asking them about the progress.

Although Hitler was seen to look outwardly calm and at ease, those closest to him had seen a gradual change in his physical and mental state. At the war conferences he was agitated and downcast, and this was made worse by the soaring summer temperatures. Due to the heat the temporary hut, known as the situation barrack, had its two partition walls knocked down to create a long makeshift conference room to allow more light and air to pass through the open windows. The hut measured twenty-five metres by five metres and was large enough to accommodate more than twenty officers for a conference.

On 20 July the first conference of the day was marked down to commence at the regular time of 1.00pm, but the officers attending were informed late that morning that it was to be brought forward thirty minutes as Mussolini was expected after lunch.

The conference began without incident at 12.30pm with the assembly of twenty-four officers. The windows of the hut were left wide open as the heat that day was oppressive and Hitler was determined to have the conference completed in rapid time so that he could meet his Italian ally at the headquarters train station.

The conference had only just begun with the outlining of operations to the *Führer* when General Fromm's Chief of Staff, Colonel Schenk von Stauffenberg, arrived in order to brief him on some new divisions. Minutes later as Heusinger was concluding his brief there was a blinding flash followed by an enormous explosion which ripped through the hut sending Hitler flying into a door and killing and badly injuring a number of those who were standing around the map table.

Outside the situation barrack there was mayhem and confusion. A number of officers in the vicinity thought the headquarters were under enemy attack. An alarm was sounded and RSD and RBB troops came running to the hut. A message was immediately relayed to the *Führer's* Anti-aircraft Detachment which manned the anti-aircraft batteries throughout the installation. Because the entire area in and around 'Wolfschanze' including the other headquarters installations were all integrated into the early-warning system they could quickly determine whether the headquarters were indeed under any type of enemy aerial attack. When the RSD received communication that there had not been any attack on the installation it was immediately presumed that the explosion was a probable bomb. As a standard security measure there was a 'total lockdown', and all gates and guardhouses were instructed not to allow anyone to pass out of the headquarters. Telephonists were forbidden to use the switchboards and everyone was to remain where they were for interrogation.

As Hitler left the conference hut shaken by what appeared to be an assassination attempt an investigation team were immediately sent out to search the site for more hidden bombs. Tanks and other armoured vehicles together with a unit of Waffen-SS troops were ordered to be brought into the headquarters to increase security.

It was not until later that evening that a report was received that Colonel Schenk von Stauffenberg who had attended the conference had bluffed his way out of the headquarters and hurriedly made his way to the airfield bound for Berlin. The report outlined that it suspected that Stauffenberg had planted the bomb in his briefcase in order to kill the Führer. Along with a number of prominent officers Stauffenberg planned a military revolt in Berlin to try and overthrow the Nazi regime. By late evening the report concluded that the revolt had been successfully stopped and the ring leaders including Stauffenberg killed or arrested.

After reading the report at 10.00pm Hitler still attended the evening war conference, in spite of evidence of his injuries. He began the conference by telling his war staff the sad loss of the two stenographers who were killed by the assassination attempt, and then turned his full attention to defensive operations on both the Western and Eastern Fronts.

It was reported that all over the Normandy sector the Waffen-SS and Wehrmacht divisions continued desperately to try and contain the Allies in check. Events on the Eastern Front were equally as grim. During the last week of July the Russians had pushed forward and rolled across the ravaged countryside of Poland through the shattered German front.

Throughout the remaining days of July and August the headquarters continued devoting considerable attention to the deteriorating situation on the Eastern and Western Fronts. Whilst they watched the enemy battle across French soil against many well seasoned well dug-in determined German troops, the headquarters was nevertheless prepared for the worst.

During the first half of August it was clear that the battle of France was collapsing. Much of the conference dealing with operations in the West consisted of ways to avoid complete obliteration. Warlimont and others pressed for an immediate withdrawal from France altogether, whilst Jodl was more cautious stating that a general withdrawal from the coastal sector would be better.

The Normandy campaign had been very costly for the Germans, with many of its elite units annihilated. In spite the massive losses, the campaign in the West had proved like the battles in the East, that they could only delay the enemy, not defeat them.

In front of his generals Hitler was annoyed by the military situation on both the Eastern and Western Fronts. As the Anglo-Americans drew ever closer to the Homeland, out in the east from the Baltic to the Ukraine, Red Army offensives had routed or surrounded battle-fatigued German divisions. In the north Hitler was particularly insistent that his forces try to defend the Baltics for as long as possible as he knew that East Prussia could soon be threatened.

By the first half of October the headquarters was once again busily monitoring events transpiring in Poland. The German Army had been ordered to defend Poland with everything they could muster. As a result the fighting withdrawal had been a gruelling battle of attrition for those German divisions fortunate enough to escape the slaughter and build new defences in Poland. The bulk of the forces left to defend the frontlines were exhausted and undermanned. With reserves almost non-existent the dwindling ranks were bolstered by old men and low-grade troops. Struggling to find more manpower, convalescents and the medically unfit, known as 'stomach' and 'ear' battalions because most men were hard of hearing or suffered from ulcers, were also drafted into the ranks. Poland it seemed would be defended at all costs, despite the age and quality of the soldiers manning the lines. Hitler was so concerned that these thinly held lines would break at any moment that he decided to drag himself away from his sickbed to try and instill some kind of fanaticism in his weary commander's blood.

As the battle intensified in Poland, the Baltic's news that East Prussia would soon be threatened caused fear at the headquarters. Whilst Hitler tried to play-down the growing concerns of a Russian invasion of East Prussia he decided it would be safer if he moved over into Bunker 11. Here in his new re-built bunker of dormitories and offices which had its own compressed air and oxygen supplies including a U-Boat air conditioning system, Hitler directed the last phase of the defence of the Eastern Front.

On 25 October as further fighting escalated in East Prussia Hitler told Bormann he would never leave 'Wolfschanze' until the crisis there had been mastered. Almost daily now there were sightings of enemy aircraft in the area around Rastenburg, but the flak positions kept them away. An atmosphere of dread prevailed in the head-quarters, especially among Hitler's more junior staff and the female secretaries. The *Führer* did what he could to assure them that the troops were doing everything they could to safeguard the collapse of the Eastern Front, and there was nothing to worry about.

As Hitler tried to infuse his weary staff into believing that he could hold back the Russian onslaught until after the winter of 1945, at the situation conferences he turned his attention to the Western Front. For some weeks Hitler had been considering a grand plan to stem the Anglo-American drive along the borders of the Reich. Over in his new bunker he had actually surveyed with Jodl the first drafts of a secret plan to attack the West. To ensure absolute secrecy only a handful of people were told of the daring offensive. Nothing of the attack was to be trusted to teletype or telephone, and the officers that were told of the plan were sworn to silence.

The offensive was known to be very risky, but Hitler and his military advisors recognized that they had no other choice. During early November the *Führer* spent considerable amounts of time working on the plan. Jodl would regularly walk over to *Führerbunker* armed with plans and other important data, and both men would work in a spacious outer room that had large windows and a view of the forest and meadows.

On 10 November Hitler signed an order to prepare for what became known as the Ardennes offensive. A week later he surprised his staff by telling them that he now had decided to leave the headquarters so that he was able to watch the Ardennes campaign more closely. Although Hitler maintained the pretence of returning to '*Wolfschanze*', he knew it would be far too dangerous. However, in spite this he ordered the construction workers to continue as though he would one day come back.

At 3.15pm on 20 November, Hitler and his entourage left '*Wolfschanze*' for the headquarters station and boarded '*Brandenburg*'. Before the train took the *Führer* to the Western Front, he was advised to make a visit to Berlin first. By 5.30am, the train hauled into Berlin's Grunewald station, and within the hour his motorcade had arrived at the Reich Chancellery, which showed unmistakable signs that it had come under attack by air raids.

Hitler and staff settled down in the Chancellery and on 22 November Hitler surprised Keitel by instructing him to make preparations so that '*Wolfschanze*' would not fall into enemy hands undestroyed. A detonation calendar for all the bunkers and huts was drawn up, and it would be left to the *Führer* to give the final order, code-named, '*Inselsprung*', for the destruction of his old Eastern Front headquarters to be carried out. Whilst Keitel instructed a group of pioneers to prepare for the detonation, Hitler hinted that before it was finally decided to blow the installation he might yet still return. It was a clear indication that the *Führer* could not bring himself to destroy the very place where he first ventured to plan and oversee the invasion of the Soviet Union. In his eyes the destruction of '*Wolfschanze*' would bring about a realization that the Eastern Front was indeed doomed forever.

A photograph taken during the early summer of 1944 showing the new Guest Bunker. In this final construction period that continued until January 1945, many of the old bunkers received additional shells of at least four metres of steel and concrete, making them completely windowless, including Hitler's own bunker and wooden annex.
(Roger Bender/National Archives)

A very famous photograph taken at '*Wolfschanze*' on 15 July 1944. From left to right: Stauffenberg, Admiral Karl-Jesko von Puttkamer, General Karl Bodenschatz (back to camera), Hitler and General Wilhelm Keitel meet between the situation conference and the Guest Bunker. (National Archives)

Hitler converses with two members of his staff and is seen reading a document. He is wearing his famous black rain cape, which he wore on the day of the assassination attempt when he met Mussolini at 'Wolfschanze' station. (Roger Bender/National Archives)

Two photographs showing the destroyed conference hut. In spite of the bomb nearly killing Hitler, the *Führer* was not perturbed and met Mussolini as planned that afternoon. He told the Duce of the failed assassination attempt and immediately took him on a guided tour of the conference hut. Mussolini was shocked at the extent of damage inside the building. (Roger Bender/National Archives/Bundesarchiv)

Two photographs taken in sequence showing Bormann, Goering, Hitler and Himmler walking along a road in Security Zone I at 'Wolfschanze' after the assassination attempt. Note Hitler's bandaged left hand. (Roger Bender/National Archives)

A photograph showing Hitler's shredded breeches after the assassination attempt.
(Roger Bender/National Archives)

Another photograph, this time showing Fegelein's shredded breeches after the bomb had exploded in the conference hut on 20 July 1944. (Roger Bender/National Archives)

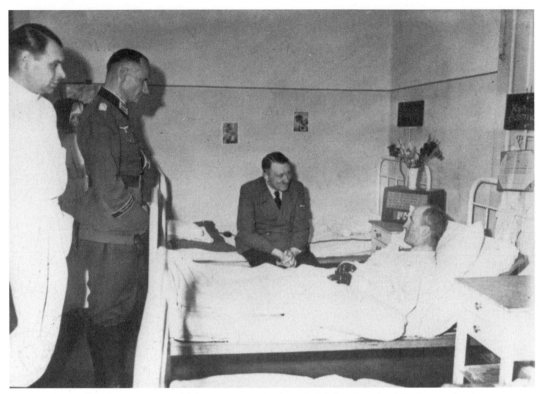

Hitler sits and comforts the wounded at the nearby hospital following the failed assassination attempt. (Roger Bender/National Archives)

Hitler talks with his critically wounded chief adjutant Rudolf Schmundt. He later died from his injuries on 1 October 1944. (Roger Bender/National Archives)

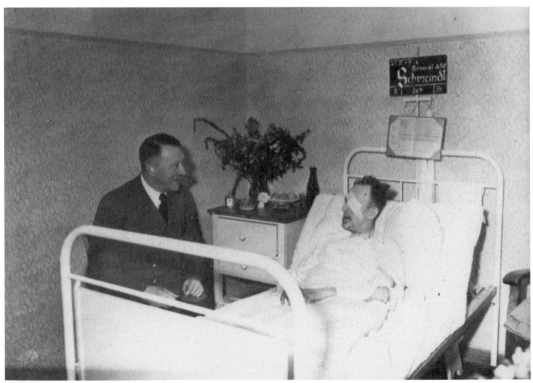

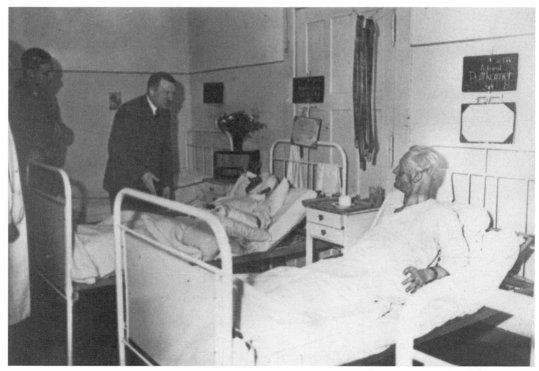

Puttkamer was injured on 20 July 1944 when the bomb exploded during the attempt to kill Hitler and was later awarded the Wound Badge. (Roger Bender/National Archives)

Hitler speaks with a badly burnt Major General Walter Scherff who was a *Wehrmacht* staff officer at the headquarters and military historian. He was appointed by Hitler to the OKW in May 1942 to compile the history of the war. (Roger Bender/National Archives)

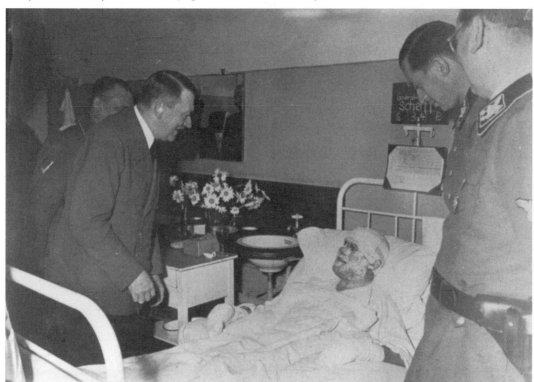

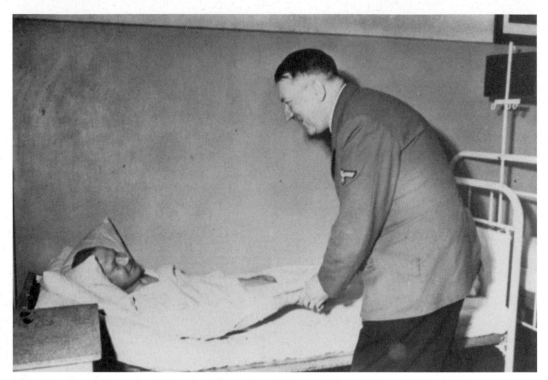

Hitler speaks with another injured staff member during a visit to the nearby hospital. (Roger Bender/ National Archives)

Another visit by Hitler to the hospital. Here he speaks to Walter Scherff, who is now on his feet and able to walk, with assistance from his *Wehrmacht* aide. (Roger Bender/National Archives)

Hitler strolls along a path at 'Wolfschanze' flanked by Bormann on his left and Goering and Keitel to his right. (Roger Bender/National Archives)

Himmler, Hitler and Hermann Fegelein at 'Wolfschanze' in July 1944. (Roger Bender/National Archives)

A portrait photograph of Hitler and Skorzeny at '*Wolfschanze*'. (Roger Bender/National Archives)

Hitler personally awards the Gold Close Combat Clasp on 5 September 1944. This was the second awarding ceremony. (Roger Bender/National Archives)

Hitler awards the Gold Close Combat Clasp to Hermann Wulf, Karl Weiss, Wilhelm Loos, Erich Carl and Kurt Ratzel on 14 September 1944. This was the third awarding of the decoration. (Roger Bender/National Archives)

Hitler and Lammers outside one of '*Wolfschanze*'s' buildings. (Roger Bender/National Archives)

Hitler, Guderain and Fegelein outside a hut at '*Wolfschanze*' on 25 September 1944. (Roger Bender/National Archives)

Hitler greets Goering. Himmler can be seen in the middle. (Roger Bender/National Archives)

On 3 August 1944, Reich and Gauleiters came to 'Wolfschanze' to show their support for their Führer. Hitler shakes hands with SA-Stabscher Wilhelm Schepmann. (Roger Bender/National Archives)

At the same event on 3 August 1944 Hitler greets Himmler, Dr Ley, Goebbels, Max Amann and Dr Frick. (Roger Bender/National Archives)

SS-Obergruppenführer Hans Jüttner, head of the SS Main Office is awarded the Knight's Cross of the War Merit Cross with Swords on 30 October 1944. Himmler can be seen present. (Roger Bender/ National Archives)

A StuG.III Ausf.G advances toward the front during the Normandy campaign. Within two weeks reports confirmed that the Normandy landings were proving successful, in spite the high casualty rate. This caused consternation among the 'Supreme Headquarters'.

Troops disembark from a Panther during the Russian summer offensive in June 1944. The third anniversary of the invasion of the Soviet Union was marked with a foreboding that not even Hitler himself could have ever imagined. During the early hours of 22 June across vast parts of Army Group Centre the front line erupted in a wall of flame and smoke. Almost 22,000 guns and mortars and 2,000 Katyusha multiple rocket launchers poured fire and destruction onto German defensive positions. By the end of the first day of the Russian attack the situation for Army Group Centre looked grim. All along the front battered and blasted German units had tried in vain to hold their positions using First World War tactics against overwhelming odds.

A StuG.III during summer operations in 1944 on the Central Front. During the last days of June the Soviet summer offensive took much of Hitler's attention, far more than operations unfolding in the West. Here in the killing fields of the Soviet Union he was aware that the outcome of the attack that fateful summer would be more catastrophic than that experienced by his brave legions on the Western Front.

A StuG.III Ausf.G advances through a village following the destruction of Army Group Centre in 1944. During this period alarming reports reached 'Wolfschanze' that the Red Army would soon be within striking distance of the Vistula. This meant that the Soviets would then be able to secure a bridgehead in the suburbs of Warsaw itself. But in spite the terrible situation left by the destruction to the centre of the front, by incredible efforts of military skill and courage, coupled with the fact that the Red Army's offensive was showing signs of slowing down, it was predicted that the front line on the central sector of the front would be temporarily stabilized.

A tank commander of a Panther V gazes skyward with his 6 × 30 field binoculars in August 1944. Over the ensuing days and weeks to come the German Army defended Poland with everything they could muster. The fighting withdrawal had been a gruelling battle of attrition for those German divisions fortunate enough to escape the slaughter and build new defences in Poland. The bulk of the forces left to defend the front lines were exhausted and undermanned.

Panzergrenadiers have hitched a lift on a group of StuG.III Ausf G's during winter operations in the East. From Hitler's outer room in his new bunker he watched the battle of the Eastern Front unfold. At the war conferences any optimism of holding back the enemy was crushed by catalogues of setbacks. During October and early November 1944 the Russian forces continued their thrust through the Baltic, and although slowed at several points along the way, they were making exceeding good progress and seriously threatening to overwhelm the whole of East Prussia.

A picture of gloom. Here a typical German defensive position during the winter of 1944. These troops are defending a line during the Battle of the Baltics.

Chapter Six

The End Comes

Adlerhorst and Führerbunker, 1945

At 5.00pm on 1 December, Hitler and headquarters staff secretly left the Reich Chancellery in Berlin bound for the Western Front. Eight hours later under cover of darkness he switched from the train to a waiting column of cars and drove to '*Adlerhorst*', the bunker headquarters built in 1940 at Bad Nauheim 800 feet above sea level, and overlooking the Western Front. Within hours of his arrival he returned to work with a resilience that even astonished his war staff. In a conference lasting seven hours his generals remarked that he was very alert and lively, inspiring and compelling and applying himself to the Ardennes offensive they hoped would turn around the course of the war.

On 7 December, Hitler finally approved the draft for the new winter offensive through the Ardennes, but made it known to his war staff that it must be kept secret at all times. Just four days later Hitler summoned the troop commanders of the Western Front to confer with him in a secret meeting. No one was allowed to know the exact destination of the meeting. Under heavy SS armed guard each commander having been stripped of revolvers and other side arms was led to an extensive system of bunkers. After being led through a number of dimly lit corridors they entered the conference room where they were greeted by Hitler who sat at a narrow table flanked by Keitel and Jodl.

In a two hour lecture the sixty or so assembled commanders were finally told of Hitler's grand strategy for an all-out offensive in the West. They all listened intently to their *Führer*, and many were impressed not only by the grandiosity of the plan, but his dynamism and determination.

On the eve of the historic offensive, Hitler held a final conference and enquired whether all the troops were in place and ready for the attack early next morning. In the Ardennes a substantial number of divisions were assigned to the area, including four crack *Waffen-SS* divisions. Although these powerful SS divisions had a higher allotment of motor vehicles they were still below their assigned strength for officers and non-commissioned officers, mostly because of the terrible losses sustained in

Normandy. But in spite of this the equipment used by both the SS and *Wehrmacht* armoured formations in the Ardennes was generally excellent, although by this late period of the war it was still in short supply.

After the conference that evening Hitler dined with his secretaries and retired to bed at five in the morning. By the time he was awakened at 11.30am on the 16th the American lines had caved in along an eighty-mile front. All along the German front from Monschau in the north to Echternach on the Luxembourg border, the cold dawn of 16 December was broken by a massive artillery barrage. The atmosphere at '*Adlerhorst*' was electric. Many of his closest staff appeared inspired by Hitler's optimism and were certain the battle was already as good as won. This cheerful mood continued for the next several days.

Hitler for the first time in many weeks was eager to attend the situation conferences and listen to the reports from the front. Within the first twenty-four hours of the offensive the SS Panzer ace Peiper continued to exploit the American defences using every means at his disposal to annihilate all enemy resistance. However, after seven days of battle Hitler began receiving increasing reports that the Allies were now beginning to recover from the initial surprise and resistance was stiffening day by day. By 22 December the Americans began stemming the German drive. Coupled with the lack of fuel and the constant congestion on the narrow roads many German units were brought to a standstill. The fuel shortages were so bad that on 23 December Peiper's Kampfgruppe destroyed their vehicles, and his remaining 1,000 men set out on foot for the German lines.

Along the entire front German soldiers were becoming increasingly exhausted. By day and night the Allied air force gradually regained control, spelling the end of any hopes for an easy conquest in the West. One crisp winter's morning Hitler was caught outside his blockhouse impassively watching as 2,000 enemy bombers swarmed eastward. Returning to his bunker one of his adjutants noticed that he seemed to have shut his eyes to the possibility that full success could no longer be achieved. His confidence carried over to Christmas, which he celebrated, to the astonishment of his circle, with a glass of wine. It was the first time Fraulein Schroeder had ever seen him take alcohol with any pleasure.

Three days later at a special meeting with his senior commanders, he admitted the situation was desperate, but he had never learned the word 'capitulation', and would pursue his aim with fanaticism. Even when the New Year arrived he ardently believed that 1945 would be resumed with fresh triumphs.

On 3 January, the long awaited news finally reached the snow covered headquarters that the Allies had gone over to the offensive with massive attacks. A subdued atmosphere suddenly descended upon the headquarters. Over the next few days the warning signs that Stalin's great offensive was about to begin caused anxious activity. When Hitler rose at noon on the 11 January news reached his bunker that the attack had already begun. He immediately made his way over to the map room to discuss the worrying developments. Two days later the situation became much worse. It was reported the German Army had been immediately engulfed in a storm of fire along the Vistula Front. Across the snow covered terrain Red Army troops and massive amounts of armoured vehicles flooded the battlefield. By the end of the day on 13 January the offensive had ripped open a breach more than twenty miles wide on the Vistula Front.

What followed were scenes of indescribable confusion sweeping the lines. The Soviets had soon wrenched open the front in Poland and East Prussia.

Shocked by the appalling losses and devastation to the front, Hitler once again reiterated that he wanted to return to 'Wolfschanze' and take command of the terrible situation that was spiralling out of control. The Führer was warned that developments in the East were now so rapid that it was more than probable that East Prussia would soon fall into Soviet hands. Despite this worrying prospect, Hitler had still not given the order for 'Wolfschanze' to be detonated, hoping that by some miracle the Red Army would be halted. Yet, he had already instructed those left at the headquarters to be evacuated, including the Todt workers.

With the Eastern Front crumbling Hitler decided to leave 'Adlerhorst' and return to Berlin where he could confidently prepare fresh military undertakings from the Reich Chancellery. On 15 January at 6.00pm he drove with his entourage to the nearby station and boarded his special train. When Hitler was awakened at 9.00am on 16 January his train was approaching the capital. He arrived at the blitzed Reich Chancellery just before noon that day.

Over the next days and weeks to come developments on the Eastern Front deteriorated. In the Reich Chancellery Hitler had decided that it would now be the most practical post to direct the war. There were many appeals from members of staff for him to move to the OKH Zossen headquarters just outside Berlin, but he declined. Many of the generals housed in the concrete bunkers at Zossen were totally aware that the Chancellery lacked any real central command structure. To them it was dysfunctional and disorganised. The increasing scale of devastation, the constant air raids and the threat of the advancing Red Army regularly endangered those that had to report personally to Berlin. The situation not only interfered with the daily running of what had become a fragmented headquarters, but made the circumstances even more difficult for Keitel and Jodl, who were compelled to commute daily from their small bunkers at Berlin-Dahlem.

Despite the unfeasibility of setting up a permanent post in the bombed Chancellery, the headquarters was still able to function and communicate with other command centres. Even with the city ravaged by war Hitler was able to undertake all the familiar tasks that he had done previously throughout the war. Here in the old Reich Chancellery building he was determined to direct the war from his desk. His presence in the city would ensure that resistance would be maintained to the utmost. In front of his war staff he reiterated that the principal objective of the Red Army was to crush the remaining German forces in Poland, East Prussia and the Baltic states.

As the Red Army ominously edged its way nearer to the Reich, Keitel had been given the job to monitor the Russia advance through East Prussia. On 23 January he informed Hitler that the Red Army were reported to be within miles of 'Wolfschanze' and that the complex would inevitably fall. Grudgingly, after weeks of anticipation, Hitler finally gave the order to blow up his greatest headquarters of the war. Once the site had been completely evacuated and files and other important data burnt, over an eighteen hour period between 25/26 January, the demolition began with General Eduard Hauser's pioneer troops sent in to blow up the impregnable bunkers.

The day after the demolition of 'Wolfschanze', General Guderain and his aid Captain Gerhardt were called to the Chancellery to attend a Führer conference to report on the defence of the East. Once inside the building they took a long detour to Hitler's office, because the direct entrance had been boarded up. Once they reached the anteroom they were met by guards armed with machine guns. An SS officer politely requested them to hand over their side arms and carefully examined their briefcases. They were then led into the room, and before they were summoned for the conference, they found sandwiches and drinks laid out on a sideboard.

By four o'clock the room was filled with high-ranking officers, including Keitel, Jodl and Goering. Moments later the doors to the Führer's office were opened, revealing a sparsely decorated room. In the middle of one wall was a large desk, behind it a black upholstered chair facing the garden. The group seated themselves in heavy leather chairs whilst their aides and lesser dignitaries either stood or found straight chairs.

Twenty minutes later Hitler finally shuffled in, shoulders stooped, left arm hanging loose. He greeted a few with a limp shake from his incapacitated right hand. Captain Bolt had never met Hitler before and was shocked by his appearance. Hitler then sat down on a chair pushed forward by an aide, and examined Guderian's reports on the Eastern Front. Uncharacteristically, Hitler made few suggestions, but did show much more interest on developments in the West.

Reports from the Eastern Front were as depressing as ever. By the time the conference had ended, the Red Army were no more than a few hours' drive from Berlin. Ahead lay the River Oder, the last major defence line before the Reich capital. German infantry and Panzer troops were ordered to hold the front against superior Soviet artillery and aviation. Although German troops fought to the death in front of the Oder, three days later on the thirtieth a disturbing report was handed to Hitler that advanced Soviets had reached the eastern banks of the Oder. Only fifty miles from the Chancellery and the Russian front now existed. The panic in the Chancellery was heightened three days later when Berlin was subjected to the heaviest bombing of the war. Almost a thousand American bombers unloaded 2,000 bombs into the heart of the capital. The raid left the Chancellery badly damaged. From within the old Reich Chancellery, Hitler and his staff hurriedly made their way down a flight of stairs that led fifty feet to the site of the deep underground bunker which Albert Speer had built for him in 1942 and 1943 at a cost of 1.4 million *Reichsmarks*. The bunker stretched beneath the old Chancellery and under the garden, beneath an eight metre roof of earth, steel and concrete. The bunker itself was not built specifically to house the headquarters, but just for temporary occupancy as an air-raid shelter. The ground measured 19.5 metres by 18.8 metres, and the concrete ceiling alone was 3.5 metres, and the outer walls 3.6 metres, thick.

There were two entrances, one from the Reich Chancellery garden, and one from the cellar of the old Reich Chancellery and the ante-bunker below. Hitler and staff always used the entrance of the old Reich Chancellery. After an air raid, Hitler would remain in the bunker until the bomb damage to the building was repaired again. Here he would sit among his closest associates eating, drinking and conferring with his staff until it was time to go back up again into his quarters.

During the early evening of 13 February, there was another heavy air raid over Berlin. Once more everyone took flight to the shelter. At eight o'clock, he dined with two secretaries, and then slept until it was time for the midnight war conference. Here he received reports that since midday British bombers in their masses had set alight the ancient city of Dresden, burning alive thousands of refugees in a terrifying fire storm. Hitler was incensed, and as he began condemning the British, word arrived that a new British attack, heavier than the first had begun. It was not until 6.15am before Hitler retired to his sleeping quarters in the bunker, wane and drawn.

In the afternoon of 14 February, Hitler and staff re-emerged from the bunker tired and strained, and began their normal daily routine in the battered Reich Chancellery. Faced as he was by almost certain catastrophe, in the days that followed his mood became defiant and aggressive.

On 25 February the *Gauleiters* were summoned to the Chancellery at 2.00pm where Hitler was determined to instill them with fire and optimism. They were surprised to see their *Führer* resembling an old man. His voice was low, and he greeted everyone with a limp hand shake, trying to disguise his trembling right hand. Shuffling across the room he took to the podium and addressed the *Gauleiters* and officials, appealing for one last effort to win the war. Everyone expected a sensational address, but all they got was a now customary oration that was both uninspiring and depressing. In conclusion to the speech he warned his guests that if the German people gave up now, they would deserve annihilation.

The *Gauleiters* left the Chancellery not knowing if they would ever see their *Führer* again. Although infused with courage and determination, many were quite conscious that the war was slipping from their grasp.

As fronts everywhere were collapsing and Germany became increasingly compressed between the Oder and the Rhine, Hitler decided to leave the confines of the Chancellery and pay a hasty visit to the receding front line in the East. On 3 March, much to the astonishment of his generals, he drove out to the front unmoved by the incredible risk to his life. Here on the battlefield, between Wriezen and Seelow, he was able to witness for the first time the brave legions of the 9th Army putting up a staunch defence with every available weapon they could muster. At Harnekop he called into the Army Corps Headquarters and also some of the divisional headquarters. Here he urged the assembled commanders to prepare themselves for the last battle before Berlin.

Never again would Hitler venture beyond the Chancellery grounds. Since late February he and staff were spending longer periods entombed beneath the Chancellery. By early March he had decided that it would be much safer if he were to move inside the bunker and direct the defence of the Reich fifty feet below ground. During the first week of March a gas protection air filter system was fitted in the bunker. Where there had been small air-intake shafts, there were now large concrete chimneys to make the shafts invulnerable to objects that might fall in and obstruct the passage. These chimneys were well guarded, along with the whole Chancellery complex.

Everywhere SS and RSD guards were seen patrolling, in the observation towers, on roofs of the entire Chancellery, and there were even spotlights installed all around. At the bunker entrance there was the largest contingent of well armed SS guards. Visitors to the bunker had to check in at the Reich Chancellery first before they were even considered a pass; their names and papers scrutinized against log-book entries. From the partially destroyed Chancellery, where long detours now had to be made, military and party officials were escorted by a guard to the bunker entrance. At every passage on their way there were SS guards, and every time the visitors had to identify themselves. At the entrance they were escorted down a flight of stairs to a steel reinforced door guarded by two well armed sentries. An SS officer took their briefcase or any other belongings and examined them, but they were not frisked for hidden weapons. Passing through the steel door they were given access to Hitler's new command centre; a huge bunker installation buried beneath the ruins of the Chancellery.

Here they descended more stairs to a narrow passageway, across some duck boards to another door, and then traversed down another flight of stairs to the upper level of the bunker. From here there were twelve rooms, none larger than a cupboard, six on each side of a central vestibule. These were lumber rooms and servants quarters, and included the vegetarian kitchen where Hitler's meals were prepared. From the passageway, which was now used as a general dining area, they proceeded down a stairway that was right-angled to a still deeper and slightly larger bunker. This was known as the *Führerbunker*. Contracted within the thick concrete walls were eighteen rooms, all of which were small, cramped and uncomfortable, and separated by an entrance hall which was partitioned into a waiting and conference room. On the near side of the partition it gave access to some offices, guardroom, the lavatories, and the emergency telephone exchange and power-house. Beyond this partition, it led to a red-carpeted main passageway which became the conference room in which Hitler presided over the daily staff conferences.

On the other side of the conference passage were rooms occupied by Hitler's two doctors, Morell and Stumpfegger, and Stumpfegger's well equipped first aid-room. At the end of the passage, a door led into a small ante-room, used as a cloakroom; and from here four flights of concrete steps climbed up into the garden. This was the emergency exit.

A door on the left of the conference room led to a suite of six rooms which were the private apartments of Hitler's. There was an ante-room, bed-sitting room, a dressing-room and Hitler's personal bedroom, living-room, and study. Inside the living room were a desk, table, and hard sofa. A portrait of Frederick the Great prominently hung over the desk. Two other doors on the left led into a small conference room filled with a map table surrounded by a wooden bench. Off this room was a narrow cupboard known as the 'Dog Bunker', and now used as a rest-room for the *Begleit Kommando* who guarded the *Führer*. At the far end of the dog bunker a spiral staircase led up to an unfinished concrete observation tower above the gardens. Labourers continued to work in shifts to complete this construction and others like it, but were forever forced to abandon the building site because of the air raids.

Apart from the Reich Chancellery bunker and *Führerbunker*, there were underground shelters burrowed beneath other government buildings. There was the bunker of the Party Chancellery, where Bormann and his staff lived with the service officers and SS guards, and a third bunker which housed *SS-Brigadeführer* Mohnke, the commandant of the Chancellery and his staff, whilst Goebbels and his staff sheltered in the cellars of the Propaganda Ministry.

The largest bunker of them all within the complex of the government buildings was the *Vossbunker*. This was connected to the *Führerbunker*, and could house up to 2,000 people. In 1939 Hitler had opened it to Berlin's hospital and welfare services. Now, six years later, it had become a refuge for injured and frightened Berliners. Every evening now a line of fleeing civilians formed in the street for access to the *Vossbunker*.

Whilst Hitler and his immediate staff were well protected inside the bunker, as a military headquarters it was totally impractical. The lack of telecommunication equipment was inadequate even for just urgent traffic, and it was in drastic need of improvement. In order to communicate to the OKH the lines had to go through junctions, and this was the only way that the bunker command centre could access the secure *Wehrmacht* communication network.

In spite of the insufficient communication problems Hitler was determined to maintain a hold over the *Wehrmacht* as supreme warlord and direct the defence of the Reich to the bitter end. From all the governmental bunkers, officers and officials came daily to the *Führerbunker* for the continuous conferences that took place in the narrow central passage. Jodl, Keitel, and Guderian came from their headquarters at Zossen or Potsdam. The air inside the bunker was stuffy despite a ventilating system hum penetrating every room in the bunker. The bareness and closeness of the windowless rooms made for a depressing atmosphere. Many visitors complained of this. The isolation was much worse than Hitler's East Prussian headquarters. At least at '*Wolfschanze*' where there was no artificial light, you could stroll through the surrounding woods, and quietly content yourself with the daily routine of work without really any threat of being bombed. But here in Berlin, this refuge of concrete, stillness and electric light, bore the true nature of the *Führer's* isolation and artificial existence, more than any other headquarters.

In this subterranean world, the throng of the military and party officials were duty-bound to watch the last phases of the war being fought out by a sick *Führer*. Clumsily and painfully he shuffled himself about the bunker, and because he had lost his sense of balance, he had to frequently sit down, or cling to the person he was talking to. His eyes were bloodshot and saliva regularly dripped from the corner of his mouth. He was depressed by his own ill-health.

With the lack of sleep his body was drained of energy. The last military conference usually ended toward six o'clock in the morning. Then, he would drag himself away and lie on the sofa trying desperately to relax and forget about the calamitous military situation. When he awoke, after three or four hours, he would once again immerse himself with the gargantuan task of fighting a war on all sides. The daily war conferences brought further disappointments and setbacks. By mid-March German forces were now barely holding the wavering Vistula positions that ran some 175 miles from the Baltic coast to the juncture of the Oder and Neisse in Silesia. Most of the front was now held on the western bank of the River Oder. In the north, the ancient city of Stettin, capital of Pomerania, and in the south, the town of Kustrin, were both vital holding points against the main Russian objective of the war – Berlin.

In the last months of the war German forces continued receding across a scarred and devastated wasteland. On both the Western and Eastern Fronts, the last agonising moments of the war were played out. Whilst the British and American troops were poised to cross the River Rhine, in the East the terrifying advance of the Red Army was bearing down on the River Oder, pushing back the last remnants of Hitler's exhausted units. The resistance of her once mighty armies was now collapsing amid the ruins of the Reich. Most of the so called *Waffen-SS* crack divisions were still withdrawing out of Hungary and were unable to be released in order to plug the massive gaps on the German front lines in the East.

One line of defence Hitler was insistent to secure was the River Oder. The new commander of Army Group Vistula, General Gotthard Heinrici, was given this task. Hitler looked upon Heinrici as one of the best defensive tacticians in the German army. Before he left for the Oder Front he had told Hitler that he had correctly predicted that the main Soviet thrust would be made over the Oder River and along the main east-west autobahn – at Seelow Heights. For this reason, he said, he would turn the Heights into a strong defensive position, order engineers to release water from a reservoir up stream, and turn the Oder's flood plain into a marshy swamp. Behind this he would construct three formidable defensive positions that would spread back to the Reich capital. The last line of defence which would appear on Hitler's situation map as the Wotan Line, was ten to fifteen miles behind the front. These lines consisted of anti-tank ditches, anti-tank gun emplacements, and an extensive network of trenches and bunkers.

Now as the Russians reached the Oder at Seelow the atmosphere in the bunker was charged with tension. During the early hours of 15 April the latest batch of intelligence reports arrived at the headquarters and they seemed to indicate an immediate assault. Later that morning Keitel informed Hitler that Heinrici believed the attack along the Oder would take place within twenty-four hours and that he would prepare to move his troops back and take up positions on the second defence line. It would be here where Heinrici was determined to blunt Zhukov's attack, if only for an appreciable length of time.

Whilst Hitler pondered on the defensive measures along the Oder at Seelow, later that day on 15 April, through the smouldering rubble of Berlin, Eva Braun, Hitler's long-term mistress, unexpectedly arrived in the bunker, having evidently hitched a lift from Munich. She had been ordered out of the capital some weeks earlier to Berlin for her safety. Now, she had decided that she wanted to return and stay by Hitler's side, no matter what happened. For the first time Eva now resided at Supreme Headquarters.

That night whilst Eva unpacked her belongings in the room adjoining the *Führer's*, Hitler held a midnight conference to discuss the developments along the Oder. It was reported that along the entire front dispersed among the 3rd and 9th Army the Germans had fewer than 700 tanks and self-propelled guns. Heinrici predicted that that the main attack would be launched in the early hours of the sixteenth and sent word to OKH that he had ordered General Busse to move his 9th Army back to the second defence line.

By 5.00am the following morning, 16 April, word reached the *Führerbunker* that the Oder Front was under heavy attack, just as Heinrici had predicted. The German troops had been ready to meet them on the Seelow Heights overlooking the Oder.

From the top of the ridge, hundreds of German flak guns hastily transferred from the Western Front poured a hurricane of fire into the enemy troops. In the *Führerbunker* Hitler was still sleeping when the Russians attacked the Oder. He had retired to bed about 3.00am and his adjutant, General Burgdorf, had been given strict instructions not to wake him. With the Red Army now only less than fifty miles away the bunker was filled with a tense atmosphere. All morning Hitler's staff paced the bunker and tried to hide their anxiety in grim humour. When the *Führer* was awakened later that morning Burgdorf told him that the battle of the Oder had begun. Hitler wasted no time and immediately telephoned Krebs demanding to be given a progress report. Although news from the front was limited he did receive news that Heinrici had been doing everything possible to hold the line. All day he had been going from head-quarters to headquarters, visiting field positions, and talking to commanders, instilling them with determination.

By the next day, the Russians had still not breached the German defences. But General Zhukov, with total disregard of casualties, was determined to batter the enemy into submission and ruthlessly bulldoze his way through. Slowly and system-atically the Red Army began smashing through their opponents. Within hours hard-pressed and exhausted German troops were feeling the full brunt of the assault. Confusion soon swept the decimated lines. Soldiers who had fought doggedly from one fixed position to another were now seized with panic.

In the Chancellery gardens rumbles of artillery from the Oder Front could be distinctively heard. Hitler's anguished staff now realized just how near the front had ominously become. Even Hitler himself began to sleep even more irregularly. His staff would often find him sitting for hours in the machine room or Martin Bormann's office with the main telephone switchboard and teleprinter units. The office was covered with maps of Germany and Berlin, on which a five-man unit marked in blue pencil the progress of the battle.

On 20 April, Hitler's birthday, Berlin awoke to a massive air-attack. Late that afternoon, wrapped in a field grey coat with its collar turned up, Hitler climbed the spiral staircase to the Chancellery garden followed by Goebbels, Himmler, Goering, aids, staff officers, and flanked by well armed SS guards with machine guns at the ready. The Berlin air was still choked with dust and debris from the earlier raid. In the cratered garden protected by dugouts and piles of German bazookas (*Panzerfaust*) at the ready, he received a small delegation of fresh-faced *Hitlerjugend* awaiting decoration for bravery. Artur Axmann, the one armed *Hitlerjugend* commander, presented the young warriors to the *Führer*. Warmly and individually he thanked and decorated them for their efforts in the now decisive battle of Berlin, and then shuffled over to a small parade of troops from the Kurland battlefield that was awaiting inspection. At 4.00pm he withdrew once more into the bunker, having seen the sky for the last time.

After Hitler had received a flurry of visitors bringing their formal congratulations on his birthday, the main war conference began. The great question answered was the imminent threat of Berlin being completely surrounded and cut-off. General Koller pointed out that the many truckloads of OKW equipment and important documents would have to leave Berlin for the south immediately. Jodl suggested to Keitel that if the *Führer* did not plan to stay in Berlin, it would be impossible to command from the Reich Chancellery bunker as they would thereby lose all contact with the various fronts. On this basis, Keitel authorized Jodl to make the necessary plans for the movement of the OKW and War Office Command, and to transfer all the remaining units still in Wunsdorf under the command of deputy-chief, OKW Operations Staff, Lieutenant General Winter, immediately to Berchtesgaden, in order to protect the operational command in the south, while the Northern Command Staff, should that same evening be assembled at Krampnitz barracks, near Potsdam, to where both Jodl and Keitel would also transfer with their lieutenants.

For the time being it was decided that overall command should remain with Hitler keeping contact with the Reich Chancellery at all times, and with the usual daily war conferences unaltered. Keitel put this to Hitler and he agreed authorizing an immediate splitting of the OKW command. Admiral Doenitz and part of the OKW staff were to leave for northern Germany, whilst another part would leave for the south. Hitler, however, had still made no appointment of where he would set up the *Führerhauptquartier*. He did give the impression that he was thinking of moving it to the south in due course. Goering, Keitel, Himmler, Bormann, Goebbels, Burgdorf and Krebs, all appealed for him to leave the doomed capital.

After the conference Bormann organized sufficient armoured transport for the convoy of lorries that was to lead the exodus from Berlin to the south. Among those to leave that evening were various *Luftwaffe* commanders, including Goering. The *Reichsmarschall* left behind two of his senior officers, General Koller, his Chief of Staff, and General Christian.

Throughout the whole night of 20/21 April more commanders and senior Nazis left Berlin to join the long column of trucks heading north and south. Himmler, Speer, Ribbentrop and many generals departed. Two of Hitler's trusted and loyal secretaries, Fraulein Schroeder and Johanna Wolf, also left the bunker. At 1.00am, after the evening conference, Hitler dismissed the two stenographers, Kurt Peschel and Hans Jonuschat, so that they could catch the night plane south. In all about eighty other staff members flew south that night. Only a few officers now stayed behind to help run the headquarters.

The next morning Hitler was awoken by news that Russian artillery had begun pouring shells into the heart of Berlin. It could be heard clearly in the bunker. Immediately Hitler telephoned OKL to identify the artillery battery position, and have it attacked. A growing sense of desperation filled the bunker that day.

At the afternoon war conference there was nothing but a catalogue of grim reports read out. Hitler was seen slumped over a map with magnifying glass and pencils, trying to deduce the next move of his enemy around Berlin. But as General Krebs started giving the daily situation report Hitler suddenly and unexpectedly jerked upright and pointed at a new *ad hoc* battle group under the command of *SS Obergruppenführer* Felix Steiner – twenty-five miles north of Berlin. In the eyes of Hitler Steiner was a brilliant commander. His desperate attack from Pomerania had slowed down Zhukov's advance in February. Now he wanted the SS commander to stem the might of the Red Army around Berlin by counterattacking. Steiner's 11th Panzer Army was to attack immediately from their positions in the Eberswalde, then to drive south, cutting off the Russian assault on Berlin. On the map, the plan looked brilliant. But it was impossible to gather forces to make Steiner's battle group even remotely operational. Steiner himself wrote that the forces at his disposal amounted to less than a weak corps.

The following day Steiner was the main topic of conversation. During the early morning until 3.00pm, Hitler had been on the telephone, anxiously trying to find out from various command posts how Steiner's counterattack was going. When the war conference routinely began about 3.00pm Hitler finally demanded news about Steiner's counterattack. But within the hour General Koller telephoned with word that Steiner had not yet begun his attack. The Russians, he nervously exclaimed, had broken through and their tanks were now within the city limits. Hitler suddenly purpled with rage. Everyone was ordered out of the room except his generals and Bormann. The rest left immediately. Once the door was closed Hitler lunged to his feet and embarked on what all surviving witnesses say was his worst rage of his entire life. In fact, his screams were so loud those living in the bunker crowded into the stairways and hallways to listen, whilst Hitler for over an hour shouted abuse at his generals, telling them that everyone had deserted him. He cursed them and spoke of corruption, treason, lies and cowardice.

Finally, exhausted, he shouted something about Steiner and then abruptly fell into his chair a defeated man. Tears ran down his cheeks and for the first time openly declared that he was despaired of his mission. All was over, and he had nothing left to do but die defending the Reich capital. Anyone else who wished might go, but he was meeting his end at his last command post.

Whilst General Krebs had instructions to remain in the *Führerbunker* as Hitler's military advisor, Keitel and Jodl left together, Keitel to visit General Wenck, Jodl to the new OKW headquarters of the combined General Staff at Krampnitz. However, a couple of days later Jodl ordered the evacuation of the barracks, having received reports of Soviet troops advancing towards Krampnitz, which was situated in the western suburbs of Berlin. The operations headquarters was transferred to a forest encampment at Neu-Roofen between Rheinsberg and Furstenberg. The installation had originally been equipped with signals and communications equipment for Himmler. From this post full wireless and telegraphic communications with the Reich Chancellery was maintained, and Jodl was able to brief Hitler by telephone on the developing situation.

Under cover of darkness, still more staff left the bunker headquarters. Hitler sent the last two stenographers packing as well; their orders were to take the last shorthand records with them. His press officer, Heinz Lorenz, was instructed to scribble down the remaining war conferences. This began at 3.00pm on 23 April, and the patchy notes revealed that the whole military situation revolved around the defence of Berlin.

Just a few days earlier the conference room was barely able to hold the crowd of high-ranking officials, commanders of various departments of the Army and *Waffen-SS*, but now most had left the bunker for safer areas outside Berlin. The only ones to stay were General Krebs, Mohnke and Burgdorf with their adjutants; Admiral Voss, the liaison to the Naval command; SS Major General Rattenhuber, head of *Führer* security, and his deputy, Artur Axmann, Captain Baur, Hitler's personal pilot, Press Chief Heinz Lorenze, Hitler's personal aide Gunsche, the military adjutants Below and Johannmeir, the two surgeons Stumpfegger and Haase, Hitler's chauffeur, Kempka, three orderlies, the kitchen personnel and one telephone operator, Rochus Misch, and with him the chief engineer and electrician Henschel.

By 25 April Berlin was completely surrounded, and the next day some 500,000 Soviet troops bulldozed their way through the city. Beneath the Reich Chancellery building the *Führer* was determined to save the crumbling capital and had already ordered remnants of *SS-Obergruppenführer* Felix Steiner's 11th Panzer Army to attack immediately from their positions in the Eberswalde, then to drive south, cutting off the Russian assault on Berlin. But it was impossible to gather forces to make Steiner's *SS Kampfgruppe* even remotely operational. Steiner himself reported that the forces at his disposal amounted to less than a weak corps. He was well aware that his attack would receive little or no support as the 9th Army was now completely surrounded and the 12th Army consisted only of a few battered divisions. As for Hitler's reinforcements they consisted of fewer than 5,000 *Luftwaffe* personnel and *Hitlerjugend*, all armed with hand-held weapons. The city was doomed.

During the morning of 28 April the Chancellery was under direct and heavy shell fire. The German command system was now chaotic. As the Anglo-Americans advanced ever closer from the west the OKW, which was charged with handling the Western Front, became terribly entangled with communiqués from OKH, which controlled operations on the Eastern Front. Communications too from the *Führerbunker* were also difficult. Orders from Hitler could not be telephoned any longer and were radioed via the communications room to the smaller of the two Zoo flak towers. *Luftwaffe* Lieutenant Gerda Niedieck, sitting at her teleprinter and deciphering machines in the telecommunications room in L Tower frequently received frantic teletype messages from the *Führer* demanding to know the whereabouts of armies and the situation around Berlin.

In the bunker there was utter confusion. On 29 April the Russians closed in on the centre of the city. In a desperate attempt to keep open a narrow route from the closing jaws of the enemy, Weidling mustered a few remaining veterans. For a number of hours German soldiers were engaged in a series of bitter and often bloody battles, trying with varying degrees of bravery to repulse the Red Army. But as the Russians isolated the city centre, Weidling was compressed more and more. The relief of Berlin now rested upon General Wenck's 12th Army. For Hitler and his war staff entombed beneath the Chancellery, Wenck had become their only hope. But over the last few days remnants of the once vaunted troops from both Busse's 9th Army and Wenck's 12th Army were not attempting to break through the Russian encirclement around Berlin. Instead they shuffled westwards towards American lines. General Manteuffel's 3rd Panzer Army also abandoned its fixed positions and was making a fighting withdrawal to the west. It too was escaping from the Russians, and its objective was surrendering to the Anglo-Americans. Berlin it seemed had been deserted by its Army, and left to the Russians to conquer.

Inside Berlin Weidling's communication networks no longer existed. Orders were now issued by word of mouth. On 29 April at 12.50pm all telephone communication between the bunker and the outside world went dead. The balloon upon which the radio-telephone to the combined General Staff had depended, had been shot down. The adjutants and ADCs of the generals no longer had any functions to perform. The shelter switchboard tried in vain to unearth as much information as possible through enemy news bulletins. That day the radio monitored Italian radio describing the execution of Mussolini and his mistress with other high ranking fascists, and how their bodies were suspended by their feet in a Milan square.

By the morning of 30 April virtually every German unit in Berlin was reported to be trapped, captured, overrun, or simply destroyed. Others were now steadily driven back towards the government quarters of the city. Russian units were reported to have already advanced along Wilhelmstrasse as far as the Air Ministry.

Hitler received the reports without emotion. He had resigned himself to perish in the bunker. Later that morning he told Gunsche to prepare him and his new wife, Eva Braun, who he had married only a day earlier, for a Viking funeral, and burn both bodies to ashes.

After Hitler had finished lunch, and his guests had been dismissed, he emerged from his suite, accompanied by Eva in her favorite black dress. In turn he shook hands with everyone, and then with his wife withdrew into the little green-and-white tiled study, closing behind him the double doors. Next to Hitler's anteroom inside the conference room, Goebbels, Bormann, Krebs, Burgdorf and Axmann stood waiting.

After more than five long years the staff at Hitler's headquarters had no more military duties to perform. Instead, they sat waiting, anxiously watching the huge electric bulbs quiver under the hammer blows of Russian artillery. And then, suddenly, at 3.30pm between the murmur of the ventilation plant and the echoing explosion of shells came the sound of a gunshot.

The God-like arbiter of life and death had killed himself. With it the fortunes of the *Führerhauptquartier* was taken and buried in the ruined charred remains of the Reich Chancellery.

At '*Adlerhorst*' on New Year's day 1945, Hitler presents *Oberstleutnant* Hans-Ulrich Rudel the Gold Oakleaves with Swords and Diamonds to the Knight's Cross. (Roger Bender/National Archives)

Panther tanks have halted on a road during the Russian winter offensive in January 1945. By the end of the day on 13 January the offensive had ripped open a breach more than twenty miles wide in the Vistula Front. The 4th Panzer Army was virtually annihilated. Small groups of German soldiers tried fanatically to fight their way westwards through the Red flood of infantry and tanks. (Micheal Cremin)

An MG42 machine gun crew in action during winter operations. In January 1945 the Russian winter offensive was so powerful that German units were simply smashed to pieces. Those units that remained on the battlefield found themselves fighting for survival with no prospect of holding back their enemy.

Waffen-SS troops on board a whitewashed StuG. Shocked by the appalling losses and devastation to the front, Hitler once again reiterated that he wanted to return to his '*Wolfschanze*' and take command of the terrible situation that was now spiralling out of control.

An assault gun crew pose for the camera inside a forest during a lull in the fighting. Over the next days and weeks to come developments on the Eastern Front went from bad to worse. With the situation spiralling out of control Hitler was now directing operations from the Reich Chancellery in Berlin.

Defending the Reich to the bitter end, a Panzergrenadier can be seen moving through undergrowth armed with the deadly Panzerfaust.

Wehrmacht troops are withdrawing across a scarred and devastated landscape and move in endless columns westward, trying to escape from the clutches of the advancing Red Army.

Luftwaffe FlaK gunners pose for the camera during the last months of the war. Note how young the seated FlaK gunner is. With the drastic need for more troops Hitler called upon young and old recruits, and put them on the front line to fight against superior well-armed and well-seasoned soldiers.

Fighting on the edge of Berlin troops can be seen digging in as the Russians approach the capital. Note the lethal *Panzerschreck* or tank shocker. The popular name given by the troops for this weapon was the *Raketenpanzerbüchse* or rocket tank rifle, abbreviated to RPzB. It was an 8.8cm reusable anti-tank rocket launcher developed during the latter half of the war. Another popular nickname was *Ofenrohr* or stove pipe.

A Tiger tank halts in a decimated German town. In spite the military reversal on the Eastern Front, these vehicles constantly demonstrated both the lethalness of their 8.8cm guns and their invulnerability against Soviet anti-tank shells.

Communication troops move through a destroyed town during a the last months of the war. As fronts everywhere were collapsing and Germany became increasingly compressed between the Oder and the Rhine, Hitler decided to leave the confines of the Chancellery and pay a hasty visit to the receding front line in the East. On 3 March, much to the astonishment of his Generals, he drove out to the front unmoved by the incredible risk to his life. Here on the battlefield, he was able to witness for the first time his brave legions putting up a staunch defence with every available weapon they could muster.

Smiling for the camera a group of young *Wehrmacht* recruits march to the front lines outside Berlin with their deadly Panzerfaust.

Chapter Seven

A Testimony of Time: Wolfschanze Revisited

Today, as Hitler had wished, Security Zone I, the inner sanctum of the headquarters, has become a tourist attraction. Visitors from all over the world are not just making a pilgrimage to see for themselves a part of history that has been denied to them, but to follow in the echoes of Hitler's footsteps and to preserve an area of land for generations to come.

A photograph of the Security Service and SS Barracks as it stands today. (Wolfschanze Museum – Kętrzyn, Poland)

The remains of the situation conference barracks where Hitler was nearly assassinated on 20 July 1944. All that remains now is concrete foundations and a memorial plaque to commemorate the assassination attempt. (Wolfschanze Museum – Kętrzyn, Poland)

A photograph of the Detective Security Detail building. (Wolfschanze Museum – Kętrzyn, Poland)

This building was home to the SS Excort Detachment and Hitler's personal servants. (Wolfschanze Museum – Kętrzyn, Poland)

Three images showing remains of the Guest Bunker. This massive structure was erected north of Otto Dietrich's bunker/office, and was known by those at '*Wolfschanze*' as Guest Bunker No. 15, for VIP visitors who came to see Hitler. (Wolfschanze Museum – Kętrzyn, Poland)

Guest Bunker No. 15 showing the flak tower and the ladder run to the flak position.
(Wolfschanze Museum – Kętrzyn, Poland)

Guest Bunker No. 15 showing the flak tower and the ladder run. (Wolfschanze Museum – Kętrzyn, Poland)

Food storage bunker. (Wolfschanze Museum – Kętrzyn, Poland)

The ruins of Hitler's *Führerbunker*. The most impressive bunker ruin of them all, the *Führerbunker*, towers over the entire forest. This huge gutted concrete building with its unbelievably thick walls and ceilings is a grim reminder of the lengths Hitler went to protecting his life from the dangers of an aerial attack. Part of the 4.8-metre roof still exists today, complete with overgrown foliage. Much of the roof behind the north face, however, no longer exists as this is where the main detonation charge must have been placed. (Wolfschanze Museum – Kętrzyn, Poland)

The ruins of Hitler's *Führerbunker*. (Wolfschanze Museum – Kętrzyn, Poland)

The ruins of Hitler's *Führerbunker.* (Wolfschanze Museum – Kętrzyn, Poland)

The ruins of Hitler's *Führerbunker*. (Wolfschanze Museum – Kętrzyn, Poland)

The ruins of Hitler's *Führerbunker*. (Wolfschanze Museum – Kętrzyn, Poland)

The ruins of Hitler's *Führerbunker*. (Wolfschanze Museum – Kętrzyn, Poland)

The ruins of Hitler's *Führerbunker*. (Wolfschanze Museum – Kętrzyn, Poland)

The ruins of Hitler's *Führerbunker*. (Wolfschanze Museum – Kętrzyn, Poland)

The ruined building which was Security Zone I mess rooms. This was situated near the *Führerbunker*. (Wolfschanze Muscum Kçtrzyn, Poland)

Security Zone I mess rooms. (Wolfschanze Museum – Kętrzyn, Poland)

The Stenograph Service offices. A team of Stenographers, under Martin Bormann's supervision, were ordered to record all the conferences that were held at 'Wolfschanze'. Each conference sometimes amounted to 500 pages each day. Every page was thoroughly checked by Hitler's adjutants, and then secretly filed away in this building.

The Stenograph Service offices.

The ruins of Bormann's bunker. This was another huge reinforced bunker with the ceiling shell measuring some five metres thick. (Wolfschanze Museum – Kętrzyn, Poland)

The ruins of Bormann's bunker. (Wolfschanze Museum – Kętrzyn, Poland)

Two photographs of ruins of the FlaK bunker that was erected in order to protect the headquarters from aerial attack. (Wolfschanze Museum – Kętrzyn, Poland)

Two photographs showing a snow covered path through the headquarters of Security Zone I. Although difficult to see in these images, in the trees there are steel hoops where camouflage netting was once attached. (Wolfschanze Museum – Kętrzyn, Poland)

Another photograph showing a snow covered path through the headquarters of Security Zone I. (Wolfschanze Museum – Kętrzyn, Poland)

Five photographs of the Goering bunker. Near to the *Führerbunker* other massive demolished bunkers can be seen standing, such as the Guest Bunker, Goering bunker, Keitel bunker, and Bormann's bunker. Surrounding these concrete structures is evidence of the many concrete-covered brick barrack-type buildings that once dominated the installation. Many of them were minded, but some were just gutted, and still stand today with trees and other foliage growing out of them. (Wolfschanze Museum – Kętrzyn, Poland)

The Goering bunker. (Wolfschanze Museum – Kętrzyn, Poland)

The Goering bunker. (Wolfschanze Museum – Kętrzyn, Poland)

Three photographs taken on the roof of the Goering Bunker. This area was where FlaK guns once stood, and overlooked the main railway line. (Wolfschanze Museum – Kętrzyn, Poland)

A photograph taken on the roof of the Goering Bunker. (Wolfschanze Museum – Kętrzyn, Poland)

Three photographs taken showing the steel steps that led to the roof of the Goering bunker, which housed FlaK guns. The author and his friend, Kevin Bowden, found this area still very accessible to the roof. (Wolfschanze Museum – Kętrzyn, Poland)

Steps leading to the roof of the Goering bunker. (Wolfschanze Museum – Kętrzyn, Poland)

Three images showing the remains of Goering's house that was constructed near the Goering bunker along the railway line. (Wolfschanze Museum – Kętrzyn, Poland)

The remains of Goering's house. (Wolfschanze Museum – Kętrzyn, Poland)

Four photographs showing the building that once housed Jodl's offices. (Wolfschanze Museum – Kętrzyn, Poland)

Jodl's offices. (Wolfschanze Museum – Kętrzyn, Poland)

Jodl's offices. (Wolfschanze Museum – Kętrzyn, Poland)

The derelict shower room that is attached to Kasino II. (Wolfschanze Museum – Kętrzyn, Poland)

Two photographs, both of them showing the two entrances to Kasino II. Steel shutters were once attached to these entrances. Note the steel hoops on the roof. Camouflaged netting was once attached to these hoops. (Wolfschanze Museum – Kętrzyn, Poland)

A close-up view of the ventilation chimney which was situated between Kasino II and the cinema. The camouflage texture is still visible on much of the brick work. Many of the buildings at '*Wolfschanze*' received this special coating to help conceal the buildings between the camouflage netting and trees. (Wolfschanze Museum – Kętrzyn, Poland)

Three photographs showing the garages, where various cars were housed, including headquarter staff, party officials, and dignitaries. (Wolfschanze Museum – Kętrzyn, Poland)

The garages, where various cars were housed. (Wolfschanze Museum – Kętrzyn, Poland)

The railway line into 'Wolfschanze'. After the war a single track was laid by the Poles, which now operates only to Angerburg. (Wolfschanze Museum – Kętrzyn, Poland)

Appendix One

Hitler's Secret Headquarters

Apart from the main Supreme Headquarters that was used by Hitler during the war there were a number of other headquarters that were not used or never got past the planning stage. Throughout the war there were some twenty *Führerhauptquartier* completed for the use of Hitler to direct his military campaigns both on the Western and Eastern Fronts. By 1945 there were numerous projects and suitable sites being planned, just in case Hitler decided to leave Berlin at the last moment. Below is a listing of Supreme Headquarters including the installations that Hitler never used. It should also be mentioned that although the headquarters moved throughout the war to Hitler's mountain retreat at the Berghof, Berchtesgaden, it was not technically regarded as a field headquarters and has been omitted from the list. The Reich Chancellery too was also not technically a field headquarters, but it has been included in the listing at the end as this is where Hitler set up his last command post to direct operations before committing suicide.

1. Amerika (*Führersonderzug*) Hitler mobile special headquarters train – 1939–43. Renamed '*Brandenburg*' from 1943–5.

[Albert Speer designs and builds '*Adlerhorst*' in 1939, but Hitler refuses to stay on the assumption that the site was too luxurious. However, it would not be until 1944 that this headquarters would be utilized as FHQu.]

2. '*Felssenest*' (Rocky Nest) initially '*Anlage Rodert*' or Anlage 'R' (Camp Rodert) built at the same time as '*Adlerhorst*' and used by Hitler from 10 May–5 June 1940.

3. '*Wolfsschlucht*' (Wolf's Gorge) – Bruly-de-Pesche in Belgium. Used by FHQu from 6 June to late June 1940.

[Another permanent installation was built in France in the summer of 1940. It was underground at Margival, just north of Soissons. It was intended to be used for 'Operation Sea Lion'.]

4. '*Tannenberg*' – Black Forest in Germany. Used by FHQ from late June to 5 July 1940.

5. *'Fruhlingssturm'* (Spring Storm). Situated in the little mountain station of Mönichkirchen, Austria. The *Führer's* special train, 'Amerika', stayed at the station and served as the FHQu from 12 April–26 April 1941.

6) *'Wolfschanze'* (Wolf's Lair). Located near the town of Rastenburg, East Prussia. This huge installation served as FHQu from June 1941–November 1944. Hitler left at intervals throughout the major part of the war.

[In addition to *'Wolfschanze'*, two other sites in the German-occupied East were hurriedly developed for a FHQu before the beginning of the campaign in Russia. Anlage 'Mitte' (Camp Centre) near Tomaszow in central Poland. The other stood west of Przemysl in Poland, and was called Anlage 'Sud' (Installation South). These were never used as supreme headquarters.]

7. *'Wehrwolf'*. Installed in Vinnitsa in the Russian Ukraine. It was operational as a FHQu on 16 July 1942. Hitler left the headquarters on 1 November 1942. He came back on 17 February 1943, and finally departed for the last time on 13 March 1943.

8. *'Wolfsschlucht* 2' (W2). This site was built near Soissons in France. It was used as a FHQu only once on 17 June 1944.

[In 1944 work began in Silesia, in the small spa town of Charlottenborn on another *Führerhauptquartier*. Its code name was 'Riese' (Giant). It was never used. Its cost, however, to construct the massive array of bunker installations was four times more than that of *'Wolfschanze'*. In addition to this new site there were other installations built, but not used. They were as follows: Code named 'Brunhilde', near Diedenhofen (Thionville) in north-eastern France. Anlage 'Siegfried', at Pullach, south of Munich. Work in 1944 had begun on 'Lothar', 'Hagen', 'Wolfsturm', 'Wolfsberg' and 'Olga'. Considerable progress had also been made on the construction of 'Rudiger', a huge installation west of Breslau in Silesia.]

9. *'Adlerhorst'* – also known as Amt 500 (Exchange 500). The site was situated near Schloss Ziegenberg, Germany. It was FHQu between 16 December 1944 and 16 January 1945.

[Supreme Headquarters then moved into the Reich Chancellery in January 1945.]

10. *Führerbunker* – The last in a list of command posts used by Hitler. Buried beneath the Reich Chancellery in Berlin this was home to FHQu from March to 30 April 1945.

Appendix Two

Abbreviations

FBB   *Führer-Begleit-Bataillon* (*Führer* Escort Battalion)
FHQ   *Führerhauptquartier* (*Führer* Headquarters)
HQ   Headquarters
NSKK   National Socialist Motor Corps
OKH   *Oberkommando des Heeres* (High Command of the Armed Forces)
OKW   *Oberkommando der Wehrmacht* (High Command of the Armed Forces;
             Hitler's staff as Supreme Commander)
OT   Organization Todt (Third Reich civil and military engineering group in
             Germany named after its founder, Fritz Todt, an engineer and senior
             Nazi figure who died tragically in an aircraft crash at Rastenburg in early
             1942)
RSD   *Reichssicherheitsdienst* (Reich Security Service)
RSHA   *Reichssicherheitshauptampt* (Reich Security Head Office)
SD   *Sicherheitsdienst* (Security Service)
SS   *Schutzstaffel* (Protection or Guard Detachment)
Waffen-SS Fully-militarized formations of the SS